Casseroles
for the
Family

CONTENTS

This edition first published 1978 by Octopus Books Limited, 59 Grosvenor Street, London W1

© 1978 Octopus Books Limited

ISBN 0 7064 0800 4

Printed in England by Severn Valley Press Limited

Meat Casseroles

A meat casserole of some sort probably provides the basis of one, if not more, meals a week in most households. They are among the most versatile dishes, ranging from a humble family 'stew' to a rather more exotic dish with wine, shallots, fresh herbs, etc. One of the many advantages of this type of dish is that it can be prepared in advance and reheated, which is of particular value when entertaining, both for busy housewives, working wives and bachelor girls. The flavour of many meat, poultry and game casseroles is often improved if they are prepared ahead of time because the cooling down and standing period allows the flavours of all the foods to become well infused. The casserole should be allowed to cool, then covered and put into a refrigerator or cold larder where it will keep for 2 to 3 days without deterioration, although greater care must be taken of dishes containing offal (variety meat).

Meat, poultry and game casseroles are also some of the most suitable cooked dishes for deep-freezing and all the recipes in this and the poultry and game chapter can be frozen unless stated otherwise. Any specific points for freezing a particular recipe are dealt with at the end of the recipe, but generally the casserole should be turned into a plastic or foil freezing container and cooled as quickly as possible, preferably by standing in a bowl of cold water. Cover tightly, then freeze. If you want to freeze a dish which is cooked in layers it is best to line your casserole with foil, freeze the food in the casserole, then take it out of the casserole in the foil. If you have sufficient time it is always best to allow the casserole to defrost completely before reheating, either in a refrigerator for about 24 hours or at room temperature for 8 to 12 hours. However, if you forget to take it out of the freezer or find you are suddenly faced with feeding six hungry people, you can place the frozen mass in a casserole and reheat it in a moderate oven, 180°C, 350°F, Gas Mark 4 for 1 to 1½ hours, depending on the quantity and type of casserole. Stir the casserole several times while it is reheating, if heating it from frozen.

Casseroles respond very well to the 'Eat one, freeze two or three' principle as it requires very little extra effort to cook a casserole for 12 than it does for four. But always remember to label items clearly before you put them into the freezer—a frozen hunk of stew is one of the most difficult things to identify!

Topside (Top Round) Slices with Red Wine

METRIC/IMPERIAL
4 slices of beef topside, cut
    1.25 cm./¹/₂ in. thick
125 ml./¹/₄ pint red wine
1 onion, chopped
1 bay leaf
1 parsley sprig
1 thyme sprig
1 marjoram sprig
25 g./1 oz. beef dripping
25 g./1 oz. flour
250 ml./¹/₂ pint beef stock
salt and freshly ground black
    pepper
200 g./8 oz. carrots, sliced
200 g./8 oz. button onions
1 tablespoon chopped parsley

AMERICAN
4 slices of beef top round,
    cut ¹/₂ in. thick
⁵/₈ cup red wine
1 onion, chopped
1 bay leaf
1 parsley sprig
1 thyme sprig
1 marjoram sprig
2 tablespoons beef dripping
¹/₄ cup flour
1¹/₄ cups beef stock
salt and freshly ground
    black pepper
8 oz. carrots, sliced
8 oz. button onions
1 tablespoon chopped parsley

Lay the beef slices in a shallow dish. Pour over the wine and add the onion and herbs. Leave to marinate in a cool place for 5 to 6 hours, turning occasionally.

Drain the meat and strain and reserve the marinade. Melt the dripping in a large pan, add the meat and cook on both sides until brown. Remove from the pan and place in a casserole. Add the flour to the fat remaining in the pan and cook over a low heat until the flour is browned, but not burnt. Stir in the stock and reserved marinade and bring to the boil, stirring all the time. Season and pour over the meat in the casserole.

Cover and cook in a cool oven, 150°C, 300°F, Gas Mark 2, for 1¹/₂ hours.

Add the carrots and onions to the casserole and cook for a further 1 hour. Taste and adjust the seasoning and sprinkle with chopped parsley.   **Serves 4**

Boeuf Bourguignonne

Made up in a larger quantity and served with boiled rice and a tossed salad this is a good buffet party dish.

METRIC/IMPERIAL
25 g./1 oz. bacon fat or
    pork dripping
150 g./6 oz. fat bacon or salt
    pork, cut into cubes
600 g./1½ lb. chuck or
    buttock steak, cubed
15 g./½ oz. flour
250 ml./½ pint beef stock
125 ml./¼ pint red wine (this
    should be a Burgundy, but
    any full bodied wine
    can be used)
1 bay leaf
1 thyme sprig
1 parsley sprig
salt and black pepper
100 g./4 oz. button onions
100 g./4 oz. button
    mushrooms
4 carrots, sliced
2 tablespoons chopped parsley

AMERICAN
2 tablespoons bacon fat or
    pork dripping
6 oz. fat bacon or salt pork,
    cubed
1½ lb. chuck or buttock
    steak, cut into cubes
2 tablespoons flour
1¼ cups beef stock
⅝ cup red wine (this should
    be a Burgundy, but any full
    bodied wine can be used)
1 bay leaf
1 thyme sprig
1 parsley sprig
salt and black pepper
4 oz. button onions
4 oz. button mushrooms
4 carrots, sliced
2 tablespoons chopped parsley

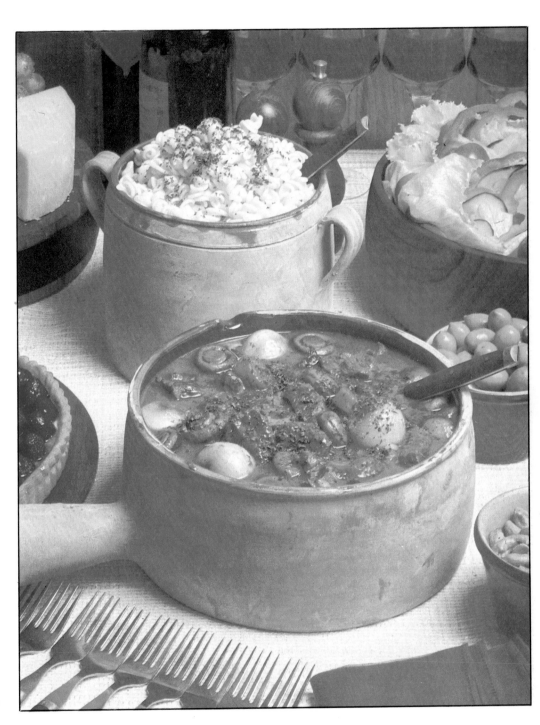

Melt the bacon fat or pork dripping in a large pan and fry the bacon or pork over a moderate heat for about 10 minutes. Remove from the pan with a slotted spoon and put into a casserole. Fry the steak in the fat remaining in the pan until browned on all sides. Remove from the pan and put into the casserole with the bacon or pork.

Blend the flour with the fat remaining in the pan and cook over a gentle heat until the flour is browned, but not burnt. Gradually stir in the stock and wine and bring to the boil, stirring all the time. Pour over the meat and bacon in the casserole

and add the herbs and seasoning. Cover and cook in a warm oven, 170°C, 325°F, Gas Mark 3 for 1½ hours. Add the onions, mushrooms and carrots and continue cooking for a further 1 hour. Taste and adjust the seasoning, skim off any fat from the surface and remove the herbs. Sprinkle with parsley just before serving.   **Serves 6**

Ragoût of Beef and Prunes

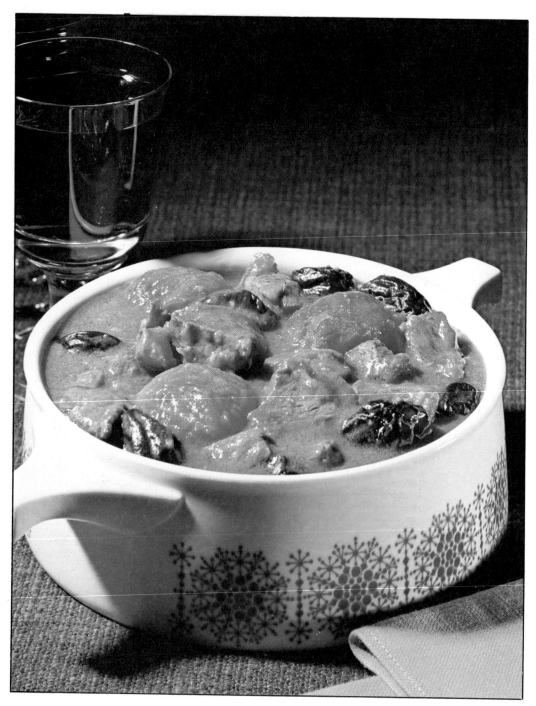

METRIC/IMPERIAL
500 g./1¼ lb. stewing steak,
cut into 2½ cm./1 in. pieces
25 g./1 oz. dripping
25 g./1 oz. flour
375 ml./¾ pint stock, or water
and 1 beef stock cube
425 g./15 oz. can tomatoes
200 g./8 oz. tenderized prunes
salt and pepper

AMERICAN
1¼ lb. stewing steak, cut
into 1 in. pieces
2 tablespoons dripping
¼ cup flour
2 cups stock, or water and
1 beef stock cube
15 oz. can tomatoes
8 oz. tenderized prunes
salt and pepper

Fry the steak pieces in the dripping in a flameproof casserole or pan for 5 minutes. Sprinkle over the flour and cook over a very gentle heat for about 5 minutes or until the flour is lightly browned. Gradually stir in the stock or water and stock cube and bring to the boil, stirring all the time. Add the tomatoes, with the juice from the can, the prunes and seasoning. If cooking in a pan, turn into a casserole. Cover and cook in a warm oven, 170°C, 325°F, Gas Mark 3 for 2½ hours. Taste and adjust the seasoning before serving. **Serves 4**

Note: *If not using tenderized prunes (which require no soaking), soak the prunes overnight in cold water, then drain. Reduce the stock or water to 250 ml./½ pint (1¼ cups).*

Rich Beef Casserole with Mustard Croûtes

METRIC/IMPERIAL
600 g./1½ lb. stewing steak
2 tablespoons oil
1 large onion, chopped
1 tablespoon flour
250 ml./½ pint light ale
1 tablespoon French mustard
1 tablespoon tomato purée
50 g./2 oz. seedless raisins
salt and pepper

For the mustard croûtes:
2 slices white bread
1 teaspoon dry mustard
oil for frying
1 tablespoon chopped parsley

AMERICAN
1½ lb. stewing steak
2 tablespoons oil
1 large onion, chopped
1 tablespoon flour
1¼ cups light ale
1 tablespoon French mustard
1 tablespoon tomato purée
⅓ cup seedless raisins
salt and pepper

For the mustard croûtes:
2 slices white bread
1 teaspoon dry mustard
oil for frying
1 tablespoon chopped parsley

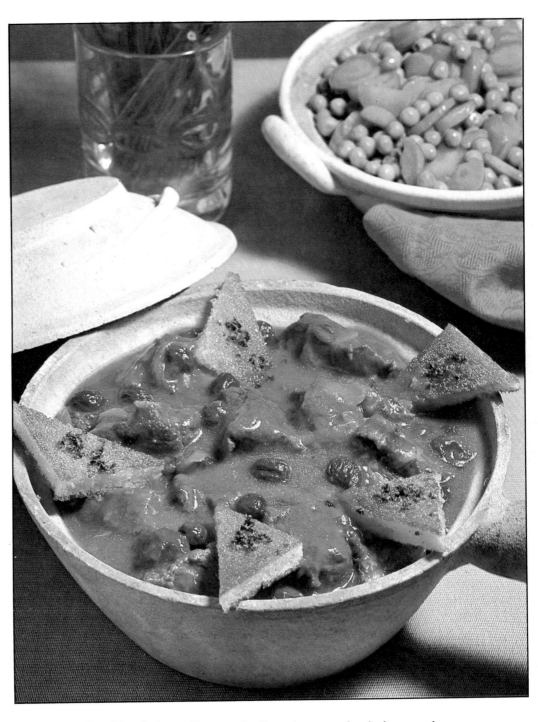

Cut the beef into 3¾ cm./1½ in. cubes. Heat the oil in a frying pan and quickly brown the meat on all sides. Remove from the pan with a slotted spoon and place in a casserole. Add the onion to the pan and cook gently for 5 minutes. Sprinkle over the flour and cook for a further 8 minutes, stirring frequently, until the flour is pale golden. Remove from the heat and stir in the light ale. Return to the heat and bring to the boil, stirring all the time until thickened. Add the mustard, tomato purée, raisins and seasoning and pour into the casserole. Cover and cook in a warm oven, 170°C, 325°F, Gas Mark 3 for 2½ hours.

Taste and adjust the seasoning before serving.

For the croûtes, cut the crusts off the bread and cut the bread into small triangles. Place in a shallow bowl and sift the mustard over them. Shake the bowl gently to coat the bread. Fry in hot oil on both sides until golden brown. Drain well and sprinkle with parsley. Serve the casserole garnished with the mustard croûtes. **Serves 4**

Note: *Do not deep freeze the croûtes.*

Beef Olives

METRIC/IMPERIAL
4 slices beef topside
3 onions
200 g./8 oz. ox kidney,
  finely chopped
1 tablespoon chopped parsley
1 teaspoon chopped fresh
  thyme
25 g./1 oz. butter, melted
salt and pepper
25 g./1 oz. flour
25 g./1 oz. dripping
6 large carrots, sliced
250 ml./½ pint stock

To garnish:
2 tablespoons chopped parsley

AMERICAN
4 slices top round steak
3 onions
8 oz. ox kidney, finely
  chopped
1 tablespoon chopped parsley
1 teaspoon chopped fresh
  thyme
2 tablespoons butter, melted
salt and pepper
¼ cup flour
2 tablespoons dripping
6 large carrots, sliced
1¼ cups stock

To garnish:
2 tablespoons chopped parsley

Cut the slices of beef in half, place between two sheets of greaseproof (waxed) paper and bat out, using a rolling pin or meat mallet. Finely chop one onion and mix together with the kidney, parsley, thyme, melted butter and seasoning. Divide this mixture between the eight slices of meat. Roll the meat up tightly and secure with fine string or coarse thread. Coat the meat rolls with the flour, seasoned with salt and pepper.

Melt the dripping in a large pan and fry the meat rolls on all sides until golden brown. Remove from the pan and put on a plate on one side. Slice the remaining two onions and fry in the fat remaining in the pan with the carrots for about 5 minutes. Add the stock and bring to the boil. Transfer to a casserole. Place the beef rolls on top, together with any meat juices from the plate, and cover the casserole. Cook in a warm oven, 170°C, 325°F, Gas Mark 3 for 2 hours. Serve sprinkled with parsley.

Serves 4

Locro de Trigo

A recipe from the Argentine, this is rather like a very thick soup and makes a complete meal with French bread.

METRIC/IMPERIAL
2 tablespoons oil
2 onions, chopped
1 red pepper, seeded and diced
600 g./1½ lb. stewing steak, finely diced
2 teaspoons paprika
1 l./2 pints brown stock, or water and 2 beef stock cubes
3 streaky bacon rashers, chopped
200 g./8 oz. red or garlic sausage, sliced
100 g./4 oz. dried butter beans, soaked overnight and drained
198 g./7 oz. can sweetcorn, drained
salt and pepper

AMERICAN
2 tablespoons oil
2 onions, chopped
1 red pepper, seeded and diced
1½ lb. stewing steak, finely diced
2 teaspoons paprika
5 cups brown stock, or water and 2 beef stock cubes
3 fatty bacon slices, chopped
8 oz. red or garlic sausage, sliced
⅔ cup dried butter beans, soaked overnight and drained
7 oz. can sweetcorn, drained
salt and pepper

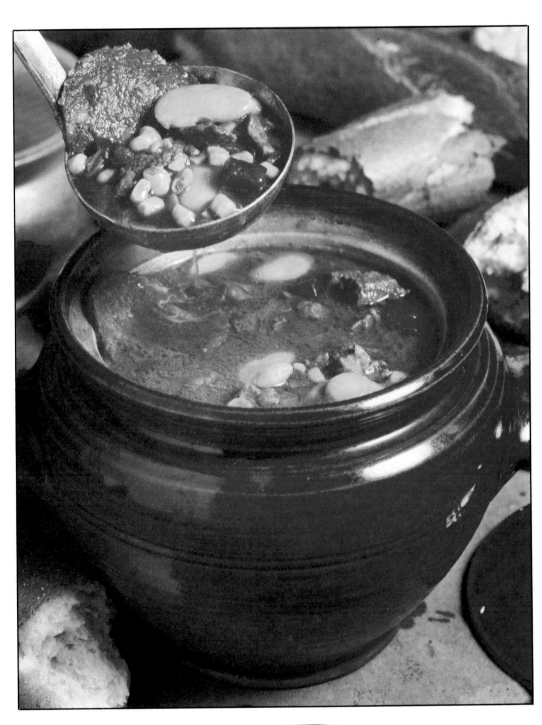

Heat the oil in a large pan and fry the onions, pepper and beef for 5 minutes. Add the paprika, then the stock or water and stock cubes. Add the bacon and sausage to the pan with the beans. Turn into a casserole, cover and cook in a cool oven, 150°C, 300°F, Gas Mark 2 for 2½ hours. Add the corn and cook for a further 30 minutes. Taste and adjust the seasoning before serving.   **Serves 6**

Steak and Kidney with Button Onions

METRIC/IMPERIAL	AMERICAN
15 g./½ oz. butter	1 tablespoon butter
1 tablespoon oil	1 tablespoon oil
400 g./1 lb. button onions	1 lb. button onions
600 g./1½ lb. steak and kidney	1 lb. stewing steak, cubed
	½ lb. kidney, quartered
25 g./1 oz. flour	¼ cup flour
salt and pepper	salt and pepper
500 ml./1 pint beef stock	2½ cups beef stock
1 thyme sprig	1 thyme sprig
thinly pared rind of ½ small orange	thinly pared rind of ½ small orange
2 tablespoons chopped parsley	2 tablespoons chopped parsley

Heat the butter and oil in a flameproof casserole. Add the onions and cook for about 8 minutes or until they are golden brown. Coat the steak and kidney with the flour, seasoned with salt and pepper. Add to the casserole and fry for a further 5 minutes. Gradually stir in the stock and bring to the boil, stirring all the time. Add the thyme and orange rind, cover the casserole and cook in a moderate oven, 180°C, 350°F, Gas Mark 4 for 2 hours or until the meat is tender. Remove the thyme and orange rind and sprinkle with the chopped parsley before serving. **Serves 4 to 6**

Savoury Minced (Ground) Beef

METRIC/IMPERIAL	AMERICAN
400 g./1 lb. minced beef	1 lb. ground beef
1 large onion, chopped	1 large onion, chopped
1 green pepper, seeded and chopped	1 green pepper, seeded and chopped
1 garlic clove, crushed	1 garlic clove, crushed
1 tablespoon flour	1 tablespoon flour
226 g./8 oz. can tomatoes	8 oz. can tomatoes
220 g./7¾ oz. can baked beans	7¾ oz. can baked beans
1 tablespoon tomato purée	1 tablespoon tomato purée
salt and pepper	salt and pepper
pinch of dried mixed herbs	pinch of dried mixed herbs

Fry the beef in a flameproof casserole without any fat for 5 minutes or until browned. Add the onion, green pepper and garlic and fry for a further 5 to 10 minutes. Stir in the flour and cook for 1 minute, then add the tomatoes, with the juice from the can, the baked beans, tomato purée, seasoning and herbs. Stir well. Cover and cook in a moderate oven, 180°C, 350°F, Gas Mark 4 for 1 hour. **Serves 4**

Note: *If you want to, you can turn this delicious mixture into a Shepherd's Pie. Halfway through cooking, simply spread 400 g./1 lb. soft, mashed potato over the top and bake for the remaining time uncovered.*

Chilli con Carne

METRIC/IMPERIAL	AMERICAN
2 tablespoons oil	2 tablespoons oil
1 large onion, chopped	1 large onion, chopped
2 garlic cloves, crushed	2 garlic cloves, crushed
1 green pepper, seeded and chopped	1 green pepper, seeded and chopped
100 g./4 oz. streaky bacon, chopped	4 oz. fatty bacon, chopped
400 g./1 lb. minced beef	1 lb. ground beef
425 g./15 oz. can tomatoes	15 oz. can tomatoes
425 g./15 oz. can red kidney beans, drained	15 oz. can red kidney beans, drained
4 teaspoons chilli powder	4 teaspoons chilli powder
salt	salt

Heat the oil in a flameproof casserole and fry the onion, garlic, green pepper and bacon for 5 minutes. Add the beef, stir well and fry for a further 5 minutes. Add the remaining ingredients and blend well. Cover and cook in a warm oven, 170°C, 325°F, Gas Mark 3 for 1 hour. Taste and adjust the seasoning before serving. **Serves 4**

Note: *Chilli powder can vary considerably in strength – some brands are quite mild, but others are very strong and ½ to 1 teaspoon of these would be plenty.*

Casseroled Steak au Poivre

The flavour of the traditional fried steak is retained in this casserole, but a cheaper cut of meat is used.

METRIC/IMPERIAL
300g./12 oz. lean buttock
    steak, cut in one piece
    1¼ to 2½ cm./½ to 1 in.
    thick or 2 thick slices of
    topside
2 to 3 teaspoons black
    peppercorns
salt
25 g./1 oz. butter
1 tablespoon olive oil
4 tablespoons red wine
4 medium-sized courgettes,
    thickly sliced
3 tomatoes, quartered

AMERICAN
2 thick slices of top round
2 to 3 teaspoons black
    peppercorns
salt
2 tablespoons butter
1 tablespoon olive oil
4 tablespoons red wine
4 medium-sized zucchini,
    thickly sliced
3 tomatoes, quartered

If using buttock steak, cut the piece in half to give two steaks. Crush the peppercorns either with a pestle and mortar or with a rolling pin on a board. Press the crushed peppercorns into both sides of the steak and season with a little salt as well. Heat the butter and oil in a large frying pan and fry the steaks quickly on each side for 3 to 4 minutes, then remove from the pan and place in a casserole. Mix the red wine with the pan juices and boil rapidly for 2 to 3 minutes. Pour over the steaks in the casserole. Cover and cook in a warm oven, 170°C, 325 °F, Gas Mark 3 for 1 hour. Add the courgettes (zucchini) and tomatoes to the casserole and cook for a further 1 hour.

Serves 2

Osso Bucco

METRIC/IMPERIAL

1¼ to 1¾ kg./3 to 4 lb.
  shin of veal
flour
6 tablespoons olive oil
1 medium-sized onion, thinly
  sliced
1 medium-sized carrot,
  grated
1 celery stalk, chopped
8 tomatoes, peeled and
  chopped
1 tablespoon tomato purée
50 g./2 oz. black olives
125 ml./¼ pint white wine
125 ml./¼ pint stock
salt and pepper
4 tablespoons finely chopped
  parsley
1 to 2 garlic cloves, crushed
finely grated rind of 1 small
  lemon

AMERICAN

3 to 4 lb. foreshank of veal
flour
6 tablespoons olive oil
1 medium-sized onion, thinly
  sliced
1 medium-sized carrot,
  grated
1 celery stalk, chopped
8 tomatoes, peeled and
  chopped
1 tablespoon tomato purée
¼ cup black olives
⅝ cup white wine
⅝ cup stock
salt and pepper
4 tablespoons finely chopped
  parsley
1 to 2 garlic cloves, crushed
finely grated rind of 1
  small lemon

Ask your butcher to cut the veal into 7½ cm./3 in. pieces. Coat the pieces in flour. Heat the oil in a large shallow pan, add the veal pieces a few at a time and fry until well browned. Remove from the pan and place in a casserole. Add the onion, carrot and celery to the oil remaining in the pan and fry gently for 5 to 10 minutes. Stir in the tomatoes, tomato purée, olives, wine, stock and seasoning. Bring to the boil and pour over the veal. Cover and cook in a warm oven, 170°C, 325°F, Gas Mark 3 for 2½ hours. Taste and adjust the seasoning.

Mix together the parsley, garlic and lemon rind and sprinkle over the top of the veal before serving. **Serves 6**

Czechoslovakian Casserole with Breadcrumb Dumplings

METRIC/IMPERIAL

1 tablespoon oil
25 g./1 oz. butter
4 carrots, sliced
4 celery stalks, chopped
2 large onions, quartered
600 g./1½ lb. stewing veal
25 g./1 oz. flour
salt and pepper
375 ml./¾ pint stock
¼ teaspoon ground mace
2 tablespoons chopped parsley
grated rind and juice of ½
  lemon

For the dumplings:
200 g./8 oz. fresh white
  breadcrumbs
4 tablespoons milk
50 g./2 oz. butter or margarine
1 egg, beaten
½ teaspoon salt
pinch of pepper

AMERICAN

1 tablespoon oil
2 tablespoons butter
4 carrots, sliced
4 celery stalks, chopped
2 large onions, quartered
1½ lb. stewing veal
¼ cup flour
salt and pepper
2 cups stock
¼ teaspoon ground mace
2 tablespoons chopped parsley
grated rind and juice of
  ½ lemon

For the dumplings:
4 cups fresh white
  breadcrumbs
4 tablespoons milk
¼ cup butter or margarine
1 egg, beaten
½ teaspoon salt
pinch   pepper

Melt the oil and butter in a large flameproof casserole. Add the carrots, celery and onions, cover and cook gently for 10 minutes. Cut the veal into 2½ cm./1 in. cubes and coat with the flour, seasoned with salt and pepper. Add to the vegetables and cook for a further 5 to 10 minutes, stirring frequently. Gradually stir in the stock and bring to the boil, stirring all the time. Add the mace and half the parsley. Cover and cook in a moderate oven, 180°C, 350°F, Gas Mark 4 for 1 hour.

For the dumplings, soak the breadcrumbs in the milk. Melt the butter or margarine in a saucepan, but do not allow it to become too hot. Beat in the egg, the soaked breadcrumbs and seasoning. Beat well together. Shape into eight small balls. Cook the dumplings in boiling salted water for 5 minutes. Drain and add to the casserole 10 minutes before the end of cooking time.

Just before serving, gently stir the lemon juice into the casserole and serve sprinkled with the lemon rind and remaining parsley. **Serves 4 to 6**

Turkish Lamb

METRIC/IMPERIAL
3 lamb fillets
50 g./2 oz. flour
4 tablespoons olive oil
2 onions, chopped
2 garlic cloves, crushed
2 green peppers, seeded and
 chopped
750 ml./1½ pints tomato juice
2 teaspoons cumin seeds
2 teaspoons black peppercorns
juice of 1 lemon
salt

To garnish:
1 mint sprig
2 to 4 lemon wedges

AMERICAN
about 2 lb. boned leg of lamb
½ cup flour
4 tablespoons olive oil
2 onions, chopped
2 garlic cloves, crushed
2 green peppers, seeded and
 chopped
3¾ cups tomato juice
2 teaspoons cumin seeds
2 teaspoons black peppercorns
juice of 1 lemon
salt

To garnish:
1 mint sprig
2 to 4 lemon wedges

Cut each lamb fillet in half or the leg of lamb into six thick pieces and coat with the flour. Heat the oil in a large pan and fry the meat quickly on all sides until golden brown. Remove from the pan and place in a casserole. Add the onions, garlic and peppers to the pan and cook for a further 5 minutes. Gradually stir in the tomato juice and bring to the boil. Stir in the cumin seeds, peppercorns and lemon juice and season with salt. Pour over the meat in the casserole and stir lightly. Cover and cook in a cool oven, 150°C, 300°F, Gas Mark 2 for 3 hours.

Taste and adjust the seasoning before serving. Garnish with mint and lemon wedges.   **Serves 4**
Note: *This unusual casserole is best served with boiled rice and a Turkish cucumber salad. To make this, peel and chop a cucumber, put into a colander and sprinkle with a teaspoon of salt. Leave to drain for 30 minutes, then mix with 125 ml./¼ pint (⅝ cup) yogurt, a teaspoon of cumin seed, a tablespoon of wine vinegar, a crushed clove of garlic and a tablespoon of chopped mint.*

French Lamb Casserole

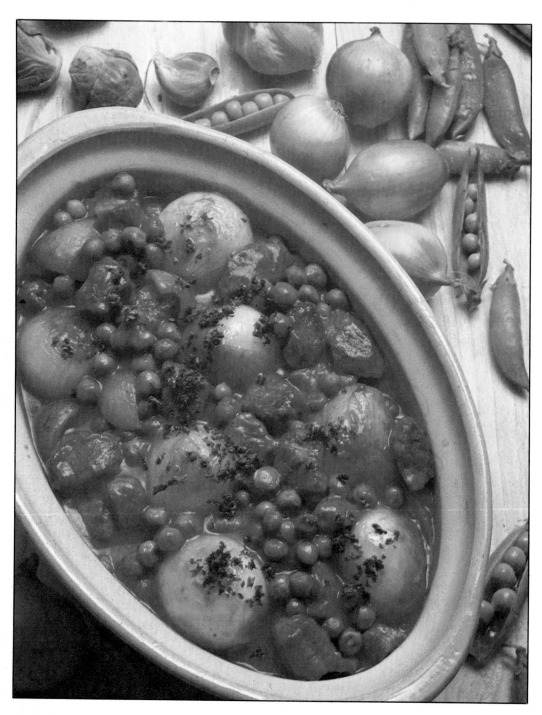

METRIC/IMPERIAL
400 g./1 lb. button onions
2 garlic cloves, crushed
25 g./1 oz. dripping
600 g./1½ lb. stewing lamb,
   cut into cubes
40 g./1½ oz. flour
500 ml./1 pint stock, or water
   and 1 stock cube
salt and pepper
70 g./2¼ oz. can tomato purée
1 bouquet garni
150 g./6 oz. fresh shelled or
   frozen peas
1 teaspoon chopped parsley

AMERICAN
1 lb. button onions
2 garlic cloves, crushed
2 tablespoons dripping
1½ lb. stewing lamb, cut
   into cubes
6 tablespoons flour
2½ cups stock, or water and
   1 stock cube
salt and pepper
2¼ oz. can tomato purée
1 bouquet garni
6 oz. fresh shelled or
   frozen peas
1 teaspoon chopped parsley

Fry the onions and garlic in the dripping in a pan or flameproof casserole until pale golden. Add the meat and cook until browned on all sides. Sprinkle over the flour and cook over a gentle heat for about 5 minutes or until the flour is golden. Gradually stir in the stock or water and stock cube and bring to the boil, stirring all the time. Add the seasoning, tomato purée and bouquet garni. If cooking in a pan, transfer to a casserole. Cover and cook in a warm oven, 170°C, 325°F, Gas Mark 3 for 1¼ hours.

Stir in the peas and cook for a further 20 minutes. Remove the bouquet garni. Taste and adjust the seasoning. Serve sprinkled with parsley.

Serves 4

Lamb and Bean Hotpot

METRIC/IMPERIAL
300 g./12 oz. haricot beans,
   soaked overnight
   and drained
salt and pepper
2 tablespoons oil
2 large onions, sliced
4 streaky bacon rashers,
   chopped
600 g./1½ lb. stewing lamb,
   chopped
125 g./5 oz. can tomato purée
2 large carrots, sliced
2 parsnips, sliced
2 celery stalks, chopped
1 parsley sprig
1 teaspoon chopped fresh
   thyme
1 bay leaf

AMERICAN
2 cups haricot (dried white)
   beans, soaked overnight
   and drained
salt and pepper
2 tablespoons oil
2 large onions, sliced
4 fatty bacon slices,
   chopped
1½ lb. stewing lamb,
   chopped
5 oz. can tomato purée
2 large carrots, sliced
2 parsnips, sliced
2 celery stalks, chopped
1 parsley sprig
1 teaspoon chopped fresh
   thyme
1 bay leaf

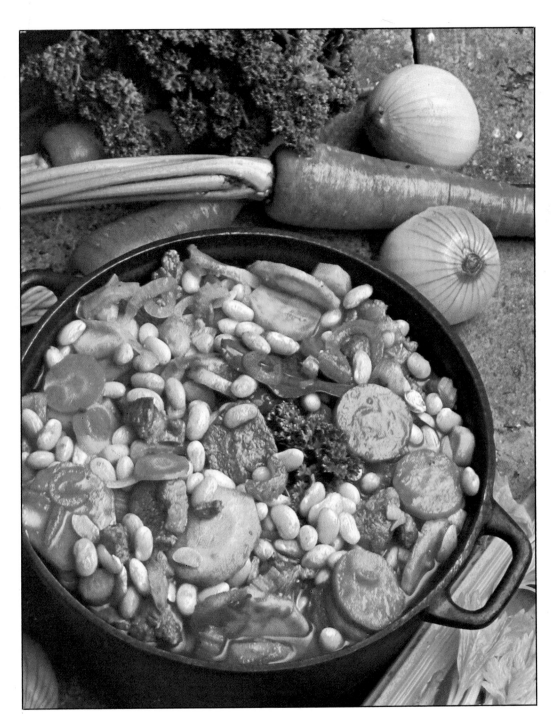

Put the beans into a pan with fresh cold water to cover and a little salt and bring to the boil. Cover and simmer gently for 1 hour. Drain and reserve the liquid.

Heat the oil in a frying pan and fry the onions and bacon gently for 5 minutes. Add the lamb and cook for a further 5 minutes or until browned on all sides. Turn into a casserole with the drained beans, tomato purée, carrots, parsnips, celery, herbs and seasoning. Pour over 500 ml./1 pint (2½ cups) of the reserved bean liquid and mix well. Cover and cook in a warm oven, 170°C, 325°F, Gas Mark 3 for 2 hours. Remove the bay leaf and parsley sprig. Taste and adjust the seasoning before serving, garnished with parsley. **Serves 4 to 6**

Lamb, Chick Pea and Bean Casserole

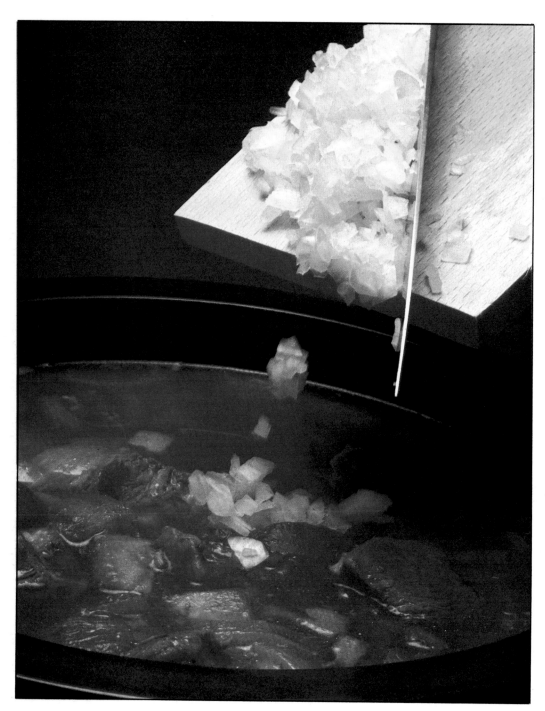

METRIC/IMPERIAL
1¼ kg./3 lb. stewing lamb
150 g./6 oz. dried chick peas,
    soaked overnight and
    drained
150 g./6 oz. soya beans,
    soaked overnight and
    drained
4 onions
1 l./2 pints water
salt and freshly ground black
    pepper
425 g./15 oz. can tomatoes
juice of 1 large lemon
1 teaspoon ground turmeric

AMERICAN
3 lb. stewing lamb
1 cup dried chick peas
    (garbanzos), soaked
    overnight and drained
1 cup soya beans, soaked
    overnight and drained
4 onions
5 cups water
salt and freshly ground black
    pepper
15 oz. can tomatoes
juice of 1 large lemon
1 teaspoon ground turmeric

Put the lamb into a large casserole with the chick peas and
soya beans. Quarter three of the onions and add to the casserole with the water and seasoning. Cover and cook in a cool
oven, 150°C, 300°F, Gas Mark 2 for 1½ hours.

Add the tomatoes, lemon juice and turmeric, re-cover and
cook for a further 1½ hours. Skim off any excess fat and taste
and adjust the seasoning. Just before serving, finely chop the
remaining onion and add to the casserole. **Serves 6**

Traditional Lancashire Hotpot

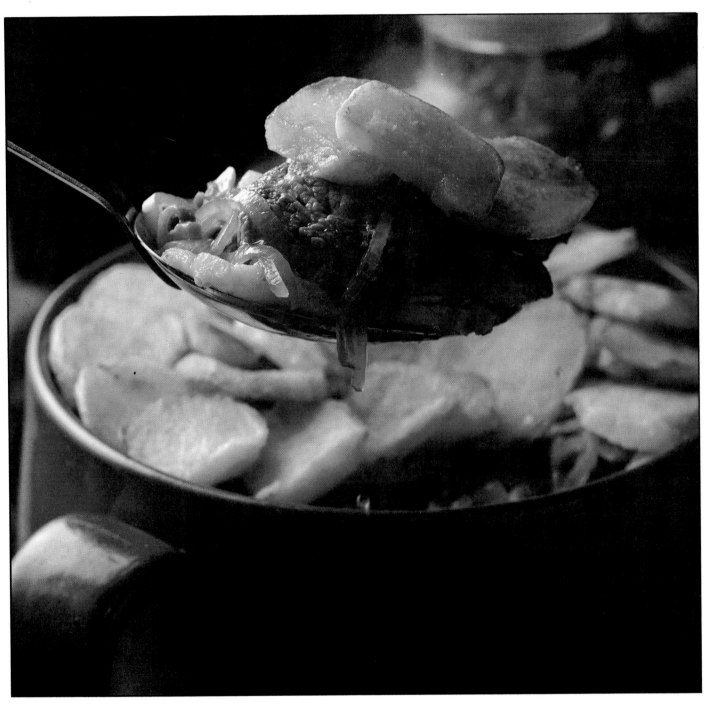

METRIC/IMPERIAL
*600 g./1½ lb. middle or best
  end of neck lamb cutlets*
1 tablespoon flour
salt and pepper
2 lamb's kidneys
4 medium-sized onions, sliced
200 g./8 oz. carrots, diced
600 g./1½ lb. potatoes, sliced
375 ml./¾ pint stock

AMERICAN
1½ lb. lamb rib chops
1 tablespoon flour
salt and pepper
2 lamb's kidneys
4 medium-sized onions, sliced
8 oz. carrots, diced
1½ lb. potatoes, sliced
2 cups stock

Trim off any excess fat from the lamb cutlets (chops) and coat with the flour, seasoned with salt and pepper. Remove the skin and core from the kidneys and cut them into slices. Place layers of meat, onions, kidneys, carrots and potatoes in a large casserole, seasoning each layer lightly with salt and pepper, and finishing with a layer of potatoes. Pour over the stock, cover and cook in a moderate oven, 180°C, 350°F, Gas Mark 4 for 2 hours. Remove the lid of the casserole and cook for a further 30 minutes to brown the potatoes. **Serves 4**

Moussaka I

METRIC/IMPERIAL	AMERICAN
4 large aubergines, sliced	4 large eggplants, sliced
salt and pepper	salt and pepper
oil for frying	oil for frying
600 g./1½ lb. shoulder of lamb, coarsely minced	1½ lb. shoulder of lamb, coarsely ground
600 g./1½ lb. onions, chopped	1½ lb. onions, chopped
1 garlic clove, crushed	1 garlic clove, crushed
65 g./2½ oz. flour	⅝ cup flour
425 g./15 oz. can tomatoes	15 oz. can tomatoes
¼ teaspoon dried mixed herbs	¼ teaspoon dried mixed herbs
2 tablespoons chopped parsley	2 tablespoons chopped parsley
40 g./1½ oz. butter	3 tablespoons butter
375 ml./¾ pint milk	2 cups milk
150 g./6 oz. strong Cheddar cheese, grated	1½ cups grated strong Cheddar cheese

Sprinkle the aubergines (eggplants) with salt and leave for 30 minutes, then drain off the liquid. Heat a little oil in a frying pan and fry the aubergines (eggplants) a few at a time for 2 to 3 minutes on each side. Remove from the pan and put on one side. Aubergines (eggplants) tend to absorb a great deal of oil when fried, but do not use too much or the dish will be greasy.

Heat another tablespoon of oil in the pan and fry the meat for about 5 minutes. Add the onions and garlic and cook for a further 10 minutes. Blend in 25 g./1 oz. (2 tablespoons) of the flour, the juice from the can of tomatoes, the herbs and seasoning and bring to the boil, stirring.

Lightly grease a casserole and arrange layers of aubergine (eggplant) slices, then meat mixture and then tomatoes in it, finishing with a circular pattern of aubergine (eggplant) slices.

Melt the butter in a pan, add the remaining flour and cook for 1 minute. Gradually stir in the milk and bring to the boil, stirring all the time. Remove from the heat and stir in the cheese and seasoning. When the cheese has melted, pour the sauce over the aubergines (eggplants). Cook the moussaka, uncovered, in a moderately hot oven, 190°C, 375°F, Gas Mark 5 for 45 minutes. **Serves 6**

Casseroled Lambs' Hearts

METRIC/IMPERIAL	AMERICAN
4 small lambs' hearts	4 small lambs' hearts
15 g./½ oz. butter	1 tablespoon butter
2 medium-sized onions, finely chopped	2 medium-sized onions, finely chopped
1 small cooking apple, peeled and grated	1 small cooking apple, peeled and grated
25 g./1 oz. fresh white breadcrumbs	½ cup fresh white breadcrumbs
¼ teaspoon dried mixed herbs	¼ teaspoon dried mixed herbs
salt and pepper	salt and pepper
1 tablespoon flour	1 tablespoon flour
25 g./1 oz. dripping	2 tablespoons dripping
2 carrots, sliced	2 carrots, sliced
2 small turnips, chopped	2 small turnips, chopped
250 ml./½ pint stock	1¼ cups stock

Wash the hearts, slit them open and remove any tubers, then wash again. Melt the butter in a frying pan and fry half of one of the onions over a gentle heat for 5 minutes. Add the apple and cook for 5 minutes longer. Stir in the breadcrumbs, herbs and seasoning. Fill the hearts with this stuffing, then tie them into their original shape with string. Coat with the flour, seasoned with salt and pepper.

Melt the dripping in a flameproof casserole and fry the hearts until browned. Remove from the pan and put on one side. Add the remaining onions, the carrots and turnips and cook gently for 10 minutes. Replace the hearts in the casserole, pour over the stock and cover. Cook in a warm oven, 170°C, 325°F, Gas Mark 3 for 2 hours. Taste and adjust the seasoning before serving. **Serves 4**

Moussaka II

This version of Moussaka uses beef instead of lamb and has a much richer topping.

METRIC/IMPERIAL

400 g./1 lb. aubergines, thinly
   sliced
salt and pepper
oil for frying
2 large onions, thinly sliced
1 garlic clove, crushed
400 g./1 lb. lean beef, minced
425 g./15 oz. can tomatoes
2 tablespoons tomato purée
2 eggs
125 ml./¼ pint single cream
50 g./2 oz. grated Cheddar
   cheese
25 g./1 oz. grated Parmesan
   cheese

AMERICAN

1 lb. eggplants, thinly sliced
salt and pepper
oil for frying
2 large onions, thinly sliced
1 garlic clove, crushed
1 lb. lean beef, ground
15 oz. can tomatoes
2 tablespoons tomato purée
2 eggs
⅝ cup light cream
½ cup grated Cheddar cheese
¼ cup grated Parmesan
   cheese

Sprinkle the aubergines (eggplants) with salt and leave for 30 minutes, then drain off the liquid. Heat a little oil in a frying pan and fry the aubergines (eggplants), a few at a time, for 2 to 3 minutes on each side. Remove from the pan and put on one side. Aubergines (eggplants) tend to absorb a great deal of oil when fried, but do not use too much or the dish will be greasy.

Fry the onions and garlic in 1 tablespoon oil until pale golden. Add the beef and cook for about 10 minutes, stirring occasionally. Add the tomatoes, with the juice from the can, and tomato purée and mix well. Bring to the boil and simmer for 20 to 25 minutes. Season with salt and pepper. Arrange alternate layers of aubergines (eggplants) and the beef mixture in a casserole. Cover and bake in a moderate oven, 180°C, 350°F, Gas Mark 4 for 40 minutes. Beat the eggs and cream together and stir in the cheese. Pour on to the casserole mixture and bake uncovered for a further 15 to 20 minutes or until the topping is firm, well risen and golden brown.

Serves 4

Irish Casserole with Parsley Dumplings

METRIC/IMPERIAL

1¼ kg./3 lb. middle neck or
   scrag end of lamb,
   cut into pieces
25 g./1 oz. flour
salt and pepper
3 large onions, chopped
400 g./1 lb. potatoes, sliced
1 tablespoon pearl barley
½ teaspoon dried mixed herbs
750 ml./1½ pints boiling
   water or stock

For the dumplings:
100 g./4 oz. self-raising flour
pinch of salt
pinch of pepper
50 g./2 oz. shredded suet
2 tablespoons chopped parsley
4 tablespoons cold water

AMERICAN

3 lb. middle neck or scrag
   end of lamb, cut into pieces
¼ cup flour
salt and pepper
3 large onions, chopped
1 lb. potatoes, sliced
1 tablespoon pearl barley
½ teaspoon dried mixed herbs
3¾ cups boiling water or
   stock

For the dumplings:
1 cup self-rising flour
pinch of salt
pinch of pepper
¼ cup shredded suet
2 tablespoons chopped parsley
4 tablespoons cold water

Coat the pieces of lamb with the flour, seasoned with salt and pepper. Put into a large casserole with the onions, potatoes, barley and herbs. Pour over the boiling water or stock. Put into a warm oven, 170°C, 325°F, Gas Mark 3 and cook for 2½ hours.

For the dumplings, sift the flour, salt and pepper into a mixing bowl. Add the suet and parsley and bind with the water to give a soft dough. Divide the mixture into eight portions and roll into small balls with lightly floured hands. Skim off any scum from the surface of the casserole mixture, add the dumplings and cook for a further 30 minutes.

Serves 4

Summer Pork Casserole with Cream

METRIC/IMPERIAL
600 g./ 1½ lb. pork fillet
2 tablespoons oil
25 g./ 1 oz. butter
1 onion, chopped
1 tablespoon paprika
25 g./ 1 oz. flour
250 ml./½ pint stock
4 tablespoons sherry
1 tablespoon tomato purée
2 tomatoes, peeled, seeded
  and quartered
150 g./6 oz. button
  mushrooms
8 stuffed green olives, sliced
salt and pepper
125 ml./¼ pint double cream

AMERICAN
1½ lb. pork tenderloin
2 tablespoons oil
2 tablespoons butter
1 onion, chopped
1 tablespoon paprika
¼ cup flour
1¼ cups stock
4 tablespoons sherry
1 tablespoon tomato purée
2 tomatoes, peeled, seeded
  and quartered
6 oz. button mushrooms
8 stuffed green olives, sliced
salt and pepper
⅝ cup heavy cream

Cut the pork into 3¾ cm./1½ in. pieces. Heat the oil and butter in a pan and fry the meat on all sides for about 5 minutes. Remove from the pan with a slotted spoon and place in a casserole. Add the onion to the pan and fry for 5 minutes. Stir in the paprika and flour and cook for a further 2 minutes. Gradually stir in the stock and bring to the boil, stirring all the time until the mixture thickens. Add the sherry and tomato purée and pour into the casserole. Add the tomatoes to the casserole with the mushrooms. Cover and cook in a moderate oven, 180°C, 350°F, Gas Mark 4 for 1 hour.

Stir in the olives and taste and adjust the seasoning. Stir in most of the cream and spoon the remainder over the top before serving. **Serves 4**
Note: *If wishing to deep freeze this dish, do not add the cream before freezing. Reheat and stir in the cream just before serving.*

Pork Chops with Cider

METRIC IMPERIAL
25 g./1 oz. butter
1 tablespoon oil
4 pork chops
100 g./4 oz. button onions
200 g./8 oz. tomatoes, peeled
  and quartered
2 celery stalks, cut in
  2.5 cm./1 in. pieces
2 dessert apples, cored and
  sliced
100 g./4 oz. button
  mushrooms
25 g./1 oz. flour
375 ml./3/4 pint stock
125 ml./1/4 pint dry cider
1 tablespoon chopped fresh
  thyme
salt and black pepper
1 tablespoon chopped parsley

AMERICAN
2 tablespoons butter
1 tablespoon oil
4 pork chops
4 oz. button onions
8 oz. tomatoes, peeled and
  quartered
2 celery stalks, cut in
  1 in. pieces
2 dessert apples, cored and
  sliced
4 oz. button mushrooms
1/4 cup flour
2 cups stock
5/8 cup dry cider
1 tablespoon chopped
  fresh thyme
salt and black pepper
1 tablespoon chopped parsley

Heat the butter and oil together in a large frying pan and fry the chops on both sides until browned. Remove from the pan and place in a casserole. Add the onions, tomatoes, celery, apples and mushrooms to the fat remaining in the pan and cook for 5 minutes. Sprinkle in the flour and cook for 2 minutes. Gradually stir in the stock and cider and bring to the boil, stirring all the time. Add the thyme and seasoning and pour over the chops in the casserole. Cover and cook in a moderate oven, 180°C, 350°F, Gas Mark 4 for 1 hour. Taste and adjust the seasoning before serving sprinkled with the chopped parsley.   **Serves 4**

Porkers Hotpot

METRIC/IMPERIAL	AMERICAN
25 g./1 oz. lard or dripping	2 tablespoons lard or dripping
300 g./12 oz. pork belly, thinly sliced	12 oz. fatty unsmoked bacon slices
300 g./12 oz. pig's liver, thinly sliced	12 oz. pig's liver, thinly sliced
1 large onion, chopped	1 large onion, chopped
2 large carrots, chopped	2 large carrots, chopped
3 celery stalks, chopped	3 celery stalks, chopped
25 g./1 oz. flour	1/4 cup flour
375 ml./3/4 pint stock	2 cups stock
1/4 teaspoon dried sage	1/4 teaspoon dried sage
salt and pepper	salt and pepper
For the topping:	For the topping:
200 g./8 oz. flour	2 cups flour
2 teaspoons baking powder	2 teaspoons baking powder
pinch of salt	pinch of salt
50 g./2 oz. butter or margarine	1/4 cup butter or margarine
about 6 tablespoons milk	about 6 tablespoons milk

Melt the lard or dripping in a large frying pan and fry the pork belly (bacon) on both sides until golden. Remove from the pan with a slotted spoon and place in a casserole. Add the liver to the pan and fry on each side for 2 minutes. Remove from the pan and place in the casserole. Fry the vegetables gently in the fat remaining in the pan for 10 minutes. Sprinkle over the flour and cook for a further 3 minutes, then gradually stir in the stock and bring to the boil, stirring all the time. Add the sage and seasoning and pour into the casserole. Stir gently, cover and cook in a moderate oven, 180°C, 350°F, Gas Mark 4 for 1 hour.

For the topping, sift together the flour, baking powder and salt. Rub in the butter or margarine until the mixture resembles fine breadcrumbs, then bind with the milk to give a soft but not sticky dough. Roll out the dough on a lightly floured surface until it is about 1 cm./1/2 in. thick and cut into circles with a 5 cm./2 in. cutter.

Remove the casserole from the oven, taste and adjust the seasoning and increase the oven temperature to moderately hot, 200°C, 400°F, Gas Mark 6. Arrange the circles of dough attractively on top of the meat. Brush lightly with milk and replace it in the oven to cook for 20 minutes, or until the scone topping is well risen and golden brown. **Serves 4 to 6**

Note: *While the topping can be frozen it can become rather soggy, so I would advise adding this when reheating.*

Somerset Pork

METRIC/IMPERIAL	AMERICAN
600 g./1 1/2 lb. lean pork	1 1/2 lb. lean pork
50 g./2 oz. flour	1/2 cup flour
salt and pepper	salt and pepper
50 g./2 oz. lard or dripping	1/4 cup lard or dripping
2 onions, chopped	2 onions, chopped
2 celery stalks, chopped	2 celery stalks, chopped
500 ml./1 pint cider	2 1/2 cups cider
125 ml./1/4 pint single cream	5/8 cup light cream

Cut the meat into 3 3/4 cm./1 1/2 in. cubes and coat with the flour, seasoned with salt and pepper. Melt the lard or dripping in a large pan and fry the onions and celery for 5 minutes. Remove from the pan with a slotted spoon and place in a casserole. Add the meat and fry for a further 5 to 10 minutes or until the meat is pale golden on all sides. Gradually stir in the cider and bring to the boil, stirring all the time. Pour into the casserole, cover and cook in a moderate oven, 180°C, 350°C, Gas Mark 4 for 1 1/2 hours. Remove the casserole from the oven, allow to cool slightly, then stir in the cream. Taste and adjust the seasoning before serving. **Serves 4**

Note: *If wishing to deep freeze this dish, do not add the cream before freezing. Reheat and stir in the cream just before serving.*

Pork Chop Casserole

METRIC/IMPERIAL	AMERICAN
25 g./1 oz. dripping	2 tablespoons dripping
4 pork chops (loin or spare rib)	4 pork chops (loin or spare rib)
396 g./14 oz. can tomatoes	14 oz. can tomatoes
447 g./15 3/4 oz. can baked beans	15 3/4 oz. can baked beans
1 onion, chopped	1 onion, chopped
600 g./1 1/2 lb. potatoes, thinly sliced	1 1/2 lb. potatoes, thinly sliced
salt and pepper	salt and pepper
1/4 teaspoon dried mixed herbs	1/4 teaspoon dried mixed herbs

Heat the dripping in a frying pan and fry the pork chops on each side for 5 minutes. Put half the tomatoes, with the juice from the can, baked beans, onion and potatoes in layers in a casserole. Season with salt and pepper and sprinkle with half the herbs. Lay the pork chops on top, then cover with the remaining ingredients in layers, finishing with the potatoes and seasoning. Cover the casserole and cook in a cool oven, 150°C, 300°F, Gas Mark 2 for 3 hours. **Serves 4**

Chunky Pork Supreme

METRIC/IMPERIAL
25 g./1 oz. butter
2 carrots, sliced
3 celery stalks, chopped
1 small green pepper, seeded
  and chopped
400 g./1 lb. lean pork, diced
2 × 21 g./12 oz. packets
  onion sauce mix
500 ml./1 pint milk
1 bay leaf
salt and pepper

AMERICAN
2 tablespoons butter
2 carrots, sliced
3 celery stalks, chopped
1 small green pepper, seeded
  and chopped
1 lb. lean pork, diced
2 × 12 oz. envelopes onion
  sauce mix
2½ cups milk
1 bay leaf
salt and pepper

Melt the butter in a flameproof casserole and fry the carrots, celery and green pepper for 2 to 3 minutes. Add the pork and cook for 3 to 4 minutes, stirring frequently. Make up the onion sauce mix with the milk, following the instructions on the packet, then add to the pork with the bay leaf. Mix well, cover and cook in a moderate oven, 180°C, 350°F, Gas Mark 4 for 1½ hours. Taste and adjust the seasoning and remove the bay leaf before serving.

Serves 4

Cannelloni with Ham and Mushrooms

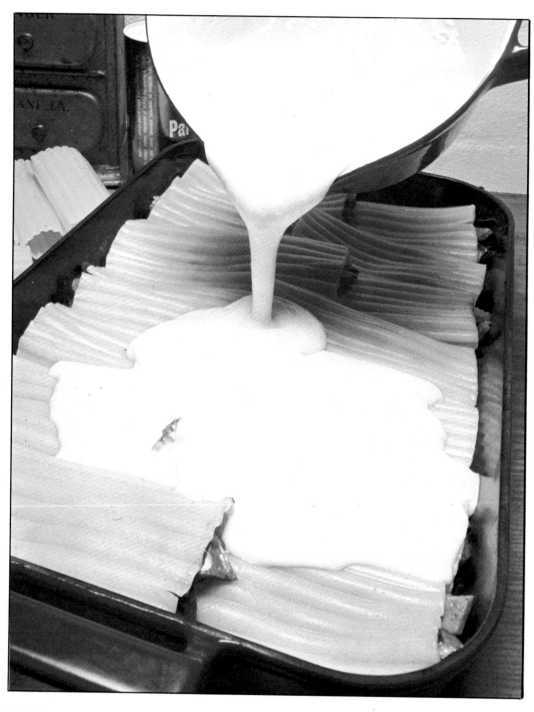

METRIC/IMPERIAL
200 g./8 oz. cannelloni
salt

For the filling:
200 g./8 oz. mushrooms,
  finely chopped
200 g./8 oz. cooked ham,
  diced
1 onion, finely chopped
2 tablespoons olive oil
2 tablespoons grated
  Parmesan cheese
salt and pepper

For the cheese sauce:
40 g./1½ oz. butter
40 g./1½ oz. flour
375 ml./¾ pint milk
5 tablespoons grated
  Parmesan cheese
salt and pepper

AMERICAN
8 oz. cannelloni
salt

For the filling:
8 oz. mushrooms, finely
  chopped
8 oz. cooked ham, diced
1 onion, finely chopped
2 tablespoons olive oil
2 tablespoons grated
  Parmesan cheese
salt and pepper

For the cheese sauce:
3 tablespoons butter
6 tablespoons flour
2 cups milk
5 tablespoons grated
  Parmesan cheese
salt and pepper

Cook the cannelloni in a large pan of boiling salted water for 10 minutes. Drain, rinse in cold water and place on a clean, damp towel to dry.

To make the filling, gently fry the mushrooms, ham and onion in the oil for about 8 minutes. Allow to cool, then add the cheese and seasoning to taste. Stuff this mixture into the cooked and cooled cannelloni using a teaspoon.

To make the cheese sauce, melt the butter in a small pan. Add the flour and cook for 1 minute. Gradually stir in the milk and bring to the boil, stirring all the time until the mixture thickens. Add 3 tablespoons of the cheese and season to taste with salt and pepper. Pour half the cheese sauce into the bottom of a shallow casserole. Top with the stuffed cannelloni, then pour over the remaining cheese sauce. Sprinkle with the remaining Parmesan cheese and cook in a moderately hot oven, 190°C, 375°F, Gas Mark 5 for 30 minutes. **Serves 4**

Creamed Kidneys

METRIC/IMPERIAL
50 g./2 oz. butter
1 green pepper, seeded and
    sliced
1 red pepper, seeded and
    sliced
4 pigs' kidneys, skinned,
    cored, and sliced
15 g./½ oz. flour
salt and pepper
125 ml./¼ pint water
3 tablespoons dry sherry
125 ml./¼ pint single cream

AMERICAN
¼ cup butter
1 green pepper, seeded and
    sliced
1 red pepper, seeded and
    sliced
4 pigs' kidneys, skinned,
    cored, and sliced
2 tablespoons flour
salt and pepper
⅝ cup water
3 tablespoons dry sherry
⅝ cup light cream

Melt the butter in a pan and lightly fry the green and red peppers for 2 to 3 minutes over a moderate heat. Remove from the pan and place in a casserole. Coat the pigs' kidneys with the flour, seasoned with salt and pepper. Fry in the butter remaining in the pan for about 5 minutes. Gradually blend in the water and sherry and bring to the boil. Add to the peppers in the casserole and mix well. Cover and cook in a moderate oven, 180°C, 350°F, Gas Mark 4 for 45 minutes. Stir in the cream and cook for a further 5 minutes, then taste and adjust the seasoning. Serve with boiled rice.   **Serves 4**

Note: *If wishing to deep freeze this dish, do not add the cream before freezing. Reheat and stir in the cream just before serving.*

Liver Ragoût Sicilienne

METRIC/IMPERIAL
400 g./1 lb. ox liver
25 g./1 oz. flour
salt and pepper
50 g./2 oz. dripping
2 large onions, sliced
2 garlic cloves, crushed
250 ml./½ pint stock, or
    water and ½ stock cube
125 ml./¼ pint cider
1 tablespoon redcurrant jelly
½ teaspoon grated lemon rind
8 stuffed olives

AMERICAN
1 lb. ox liver
¼ cup flour
salt and pepper
¼ cup dripping
2 large onions, sliced
2 garlic cloves, crushed
1¼ cups stock, or water and
    ½ stock cube
⅝ cup cider
1 tablespoon redcurrant jelly
½ teaspoon grated lemon rind
8 stuffed olives

Cut the liver into narrow strips and coat with the flour, seasoned with salt and pepper. Heat the dripping in a large frying pan, add the liver and cook quickly on all sides for a few minutes. Remove from the pan and place in a casserole. Add the onions and garlic and fry gently for 5 minutes. Sprinkle over any remaining flour and cook for 1 minute. Gradually blend in the stock or water and stock cube and cider and bring to the boil, stirring all the time. Add the redcurrant jelly and lemon rind, pour over the liver in the casserole and cover tightly with a lid.

Cook in a warm oven, 170°C, 325°F, Gas Mark 3 for 30 minutes. Just before serving, stir in the olives.   **Serves 4**

Oxtail with Grapes

In both this and the recipe for Oxtail with Black Olives it is best if you can make the dish the day before, leave it to cool, and then refrigerate it overnight so that all the excess fat can easily be removed from the top.

METRIC/IMPERIAL	AMERICAN
2 medium-sized to large oxtails, cut in 5 cm./2 in. pieces	*2 medium-sized to large oxtails, cut in 2 in. pieces*
4 to 5 streaky bacon rashers, chopped	*4 to 5 fatty bacon slices, chopped*
2 large onions, chopped	*2 large onions, chopped*
2 garlic cloves, crushed	*2 garlic cloves, crushed*
4 large carrots, sliced	*4 large carrots, sliced*
2 bay leaves	*2 bay leaves*
1 parsley sprig	*1 parsley sprig*
1 thyme sprig	*1 thyme sprig*
salt and pepper	*salt and pepper*
800 g./2 lb. seedless white grapes	*2 lb. seedless white grapes*

Cut off any excess fat from the oxtails and soak them for about 3 hours in cold water to allow the blood to drain out. Drain and dry well.

Fry the bacon in a large flameproof casserole over a gentle heat until the fat runs out. Add the onions, garlic and carrots and fry gently, stirring a few times, for about 10 minutes. Add the oxtail, together with the bay leaves, parsley, thyme and seasoning and cook for a further 20 minutes, stirring from time to time. Take the grapes off the stalks and crush them lightly in a bowl. Add to the casserole, cover with a sheet of foil, then the lid and transfer to a cool oven, 150°C, 300°F, Gas Mark 2 to cook for 4 hours.

Remove from the oven, allow to cool, then skim off all the excess fat. Take all the meat off the bones and place in a casserole or saucepan with the carrots. Push the sauce through a strainer or put into a liquidizer and blend for a minute, then pour over the meat. Reheat gently either on top of the stove or in a moderate oven, 180°C, 350°F, Gas Mark 4 for 35 to 45 minutes. Skim off all excess fat before serving. **Serves 8**

Oxtail with Black Olives

METRIC/IMPERIAL	AMERICAN
2 medium-sized oxtails, cut in 5 cm./2 in. pieces	*2 medium-sized oxtails, cut in 2 in. pieces*
2 tablespoons olive oil	*2 tablespoons olive oil*
4 tablespoons brandy	*4 tablespoons brandy*
250 ml./½ pint white wine stock or water	*1¼ cups white wine stock or water*
2 garlic cloves, crushed	*2 garlic cloves, crushed*
finely pared rind of ½ small orange	*finely pared rind of ½ small orange*
1 bouquet garni	*1 bouquet garni*
100 g./4 oz. black olives, stoned	*4 oz. black olives, pitted*
25 g./1 oz. butter	*2 tablespoons butter*
25 g./1 oz. flour	*¼ cup flour*

Cut off any excess fat from the oxtails and soak them for about 3 hours in cold water to allow the blood to drain out. Drain and dry well.

Heat the oil in a large flameproof casserole, add a few pieces of oxtail at a time and fry until brown all over. Return all the oxtail to the casserole. Warm the brandy in a small pan, ignite and pour over the oxtail. Do this very carefully as the flames can leap quite high. When the flames have died down, add the wine and let it boil rapidly for a few minutes. Add just enough stock or water to cover the oxtail, with the garlic, orange rind and bouquet garni. Cover the casserole and cook in a cool oven, 150°C, 300°F, Gas Mark 2 for 3 hours. Pour the liquid off into a bowl, discard the orange rind and bouquet garni and refrigerate the liquid and meat separately overnight.

The following day, skim off all the excess fat from the liquid. Turn into a pan with the oxtail and the olives and cook on top of the stove for a further 1 to 1½ hours or until the meat comes easily away from the bones. Blend the butter and flour together until they form a smooth paste. Add to the simmering liquid a teaspoon at a time, stirring well between each addition. Allow to simmer for a further 5 minutes, then serve with boiled rice. **Serves 8**

Poultry & Game Casseroles

There are two very good points in favour of casseroling poultry; first, long, slow cooking with herbs and spices adds flavour to today's rather flavourless battery chickens, and second, it enables you to make use of boiling chickens which are usually cheaper and have more flavour. Apart from one recipe, I have assumed that most people will be using chicken joints (pieces) or younger roasting chicken, but boiling chicken can always be used provided that the cooking time is increased by about 2 hours.

Some people feel that it is a sacrilege to casserole a game bird and, particularly if one is not lucky enough to eat game very often, nothing is nicer than a roasted pheasant or grouse. However, if the bird is of dubious age I think it is better to serve it tender in a casserole than roasted and tough. It is sometimes possible to buy game birds which are sold specifically for casseroling and these are much cheaper than the roasting birds.

Chicken Curry with Yogurt

METRIC/IMPERIAL	AMERICAN
4 chicken breasts	4 chicken breasts
1 teaspoon ground turmeric	1 teaspoon ground turmeric
1 teaspoon ground cumin	1 teaspoon ground cumin
1 garlic clove, crushed	1 garlic clove, crushed
250 ml./½ pint natural yogurt	1¼ cups natural yogurt
25 g./1 oz. butter	2 tablespoons butter
1 onion, sliced	1 onion, sliced
¼ teaspoon ground cloves	¼ teaspoon ground cloves
1 teaspoon ground cinnamon	1 teaspoon ground cinnamon
salt	salt

Remove the skin and bone from the chicken breasts, cut into bite-sized pieces and place in a shallow dish. Blend the turmeric, cumin, garlic and two-thirds of the yogurt together. Pour over the chicken and leave to marinate for 1 hour.

Melt the butter in a flameproof casserole and gently fry the onion for 5 minutes until golden. Add the cloves and cinnamon and fry for a further 2 to 3 minutes. Add the meat together with the marinade and a little salt. Cover and cook in a warm oven, 170°C, 325°F, Gas Mark 3 for 1½ hours. Stir in the extra yogurt just before serving and taste and adjust the seasoning. **Serves 4**

Note: *Do not deep freeze this dish.*

Chicken and Peanut Casserole

METRIC/IMPERIAL	AMERICAN
1¼ kg./3 lb. chicken	3 lb. chicken
50 g./2 oz. butter	¼ cup butter
1 onion, chopped	1 onion, chopped
25 g./1 oz. flour	¼ cup flour
3 tablespoons crunchy peanut butter	3 tablespoons crunchy peanut butter
375 ml./¾ pint milk	2 cups milk
salt and pepper	salt and pepper
50 g./2 oz. salted peanuts	¼ cup salted peanuts
25 g./1 oz. fresh white breadcrumbs	½ cup fresh white breadcrumbs

Cut the chicken into joints (pieces). Melt the butter in a large pan and fry the chicken on all sides until golden brown. Remove from the pan and place in a casserole. Add the onion to the pan and cook for 5 minutes. Stir in the flour and cook for 2 minutes, then remove from the heat and stir in the peanut butter and milk. Return to the heat and bring to the boil, stirring all the time. Season and pour over the chicken in the casserole. Cover and cook in a moderately hot oven, 190°C, 375°F, Gas Mark 5 for 1 hour. Remove the lid, sprinkle with the peanuts and breadcrumbs and bake uncovered for a further 10 minutes. **Serves 4 to 6**

Note: *If wishing to deep freeze this dish, do not add the topping until reheating.*

Chicken with Apricots

METRIC/IMPERIAL
200 g./8 oz. dried apricots
25 g./1 oz. butter
2 tablespoons oil
1¼ kg./3 lb. chicken, cut into
*   serving pieces*
1 onion, chopped
25 g./1 oz. flour
salt and pepper
1 bouquet garni
sugar (optional)
1 parsley sprig

AMERICAN
1⅓ cups dried apricots
2 tablespoons butter
2 tablespoons oil
3 lb. chicken, cut into
*   serving pieces*
1 onion, chopped
¼ cup flour
salt and pepper
1 bouquet garni
sugar (optional)
1 parsley sprig

Cover the apricots with cold water and leave to soak overnight. Drain, reserving the soaking liquid. Make it up to 500 ml./1 pint (2½ cups) with water, if necessary. Heat the butter and oil in a pan. Fry the chicken pieces on all sides until golden brown. Remove from the pan and place in a casserole. Fry the onion in the fat remaining in the pan for 5 minutes. Sprinkle in the flour and cook for 2 minutes, stirring constantly. Gradually stir in the apricot liquid, then bring to the boil, stirring all the time. Add the apricots, seasoning and bouquet garni. Pour over the chicken in the casserole. Cover and cook in a moderate oven, 180°C, 350°F, Gas Mark 4 for 1 hour. Taste and adjust the seasoning and remove the bouquet garni. Add a little sugar if wished, and serve garnished with parsley.

Serves 6

Mild Chicken Curry

METRIC/IMPERIAL
1¼ kg./3 lb. chicken
4 tablespoons oil
2 onions, chopped
25 g./1 oz. flour
1 tablespoon curry powder
250 ml./½ pint chicken stock,
    or water and 1 chicken
    stock cube
1 tablespoon mango chutney
1 tablespoon cherry jam
salt and pepper
2 tablespoons sultanas
1 dessert apple, cored and
    chopped
few lemon wedges

AMERICAN
3 lb. chicken
4 tablespoons oil
2 onions, chopped
¼ cup flour
1 tablespoon curry powder
1¼ cups chicken stock, or
    water and 1 chicken stock
    cube
1 tablespoon mango chutney
1 tablespoon cherry jam
salt and pepper
2 tablespoons seedless
    raisins
1 dessert apple, cored and
    chopped
few lemon wedges

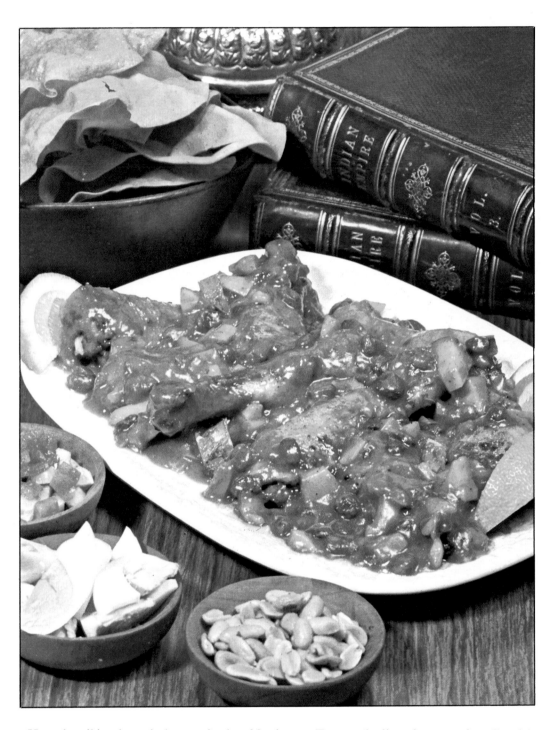

Cut the chicken into eight pieces. Heat the oil in a large frying pan, add the chicken pieces and fry until golden brown on all sides. Remove from the pan and place in a casserole. Fry the onions in the oil remaining in the pan until soft. Blend in the flour and curry powder and cook for 1 minute. Gradually add the stock, or water and stock cube, then bring to the boil, stirring all the time. Add the chutney, jam and seasoning and pour over the chicken in the casserole. Cover and cook in a warm oven, 170°C, 325°F, Gas Mark 3 for 45 minutes.

Add the sultanas (raisins) and apple and cook, covered, for a further 30 minutes. Taste and adjust the seasoning. Garnish with lemon wedges and serve with boiled rice, poppadums, peanuts, wedges of hard-boiled egg and chopped cucumber and tomato. **Serves 4**

Chicken Paprika

METRIC/IMPERIAL	AMERICAN
50 g./2 oz. butter	1/4 cup butter
2 tablespoons oil	2 tablespoons oil
4 chicken joints	4 chicken pieces
25 g./1 oz. flour	1/4 cup flour
2 tablespoons paprika	2 tablespoons paprika
500 ml./1 pint chicken stock, or water and 1 chicken stock cube	2 1/2 cups chicken stock, or water and 1 chicken stock cube
2 tablespoons redcurrant jelly	2 tablespoons redcurrant jelly
finely pared rind of 1 lemon	finely pared rind of 1 lemon
1 thyme sprig	1 thyme sprig
1 parsley sprig	1 parsley sprig
100 g./4 oz. button mushrooms	4 oz. button mushrooms
125 ml./1/4 pint soured cream	5/8 cup sour cream

Heat the butter and oil in a frying pan and fry the chicken joints (pieces) on all sides until golden brown. Remove from the pan and place in a casserole. Stir the flour and paprika into the fat remaining in the pan and cook gently for 2 to 3 minutes. Gradually stir in the stock or water and stock cube and the redcurrant jelly and bring to the boil, stirring all the time. Pour over the chicken in the casserole. Tie the lemon rind, thyme and parsley together with a piece of thread and add to the chicken with the mushrooms. Cover and cook in a moderate oven, 180°C, 350°F, Gas Mark 4 for 1 1/2 hours.

Remove the lemon rind, thyme and parsley. Taste and adjust the seasoning and pile the soured cream in the centre just before serving. **Serves 4**

Note: *If wishing to freeze, do not add the soured cream. Freeze, then reheat and add the soured cream just before serving.*

Chicken and Avocado Casserole

METRIC/IMPERIAL
6 chicken joints
40 g./1¹/₂ oz. flour
salt and pepper
1 tablespoon chopped fresh
 thyme
grated rind and juice of
 1 lemon
50 g./2 oz. butter
2 onions, chopped
250 ml./¹/₂ pint white wine
125 ml./¹/₄ pint chicken stock
125 ml./¹/₄ pint soured cream
2 avocado pears, peeled,
 stoned and sliced

AMERICAN
6 chicken pieces
6 tablespoons flour
salt and pepper
1 tablespoon chopped fresh
 thyme
grated rind and juice of
 1 lemon
¹/₄ cup butter
2 onions, chopped
1¹/₄ cups white wine
⁵/₈ cup chicken stock
⁵/₈ cup sour cream
2 avocados, peeled, stoned
 and sliced

Coat the chicken joints (pieces) with the flour, seasoned with salt and pepper, the chopped thyme and lemon rind. Melt the butter in a large frying pan and fry the chicken joints (pieces) on all sides until golden brown. Remove from the pan and place in a casserole. Fry the onions in the fat remaining in the pan for about 5 minutes. Sprinkle over any remaining flour, cook for 1 minute, then gradually stir in the wine and stock. Bring to the boil, stirring all the time. Pour over the chicken in the casserole, cover and cook in a moderate oven, 180°C, 350°F, Gas Mark 4 for 1 hour.

Remove the casserole from the oven, allow to cool for a minute, then stir in the soured cream. Toss the avocado slices in the lemon juice. Add to the chicken, cover the casserole and return to the oven for a further 10 minutes.   **Serves 6**

Note: *Do not freeze this dish after the cream and avocado pears have been added. If wishing to freeze, cook for 1 hour then freeze. Reheat and then add the soured cream and avocado pears as above.*

Chicken with Apples and Cider

METRIC/IMPERIAL	AMERICAN
200 g./4 oz. butter	½ cup butter
1¼ kg./3 lb. chicken, cut into serving pieces	3 lb. chicken, cut into serving pieces
6 dessert apples	6 dessert apples
salt and freshly ground black pepper	salt and freshly ground black pepper
25 g./1 oz. flour	¼ cup flour
375 ml./¾ pint cider	2 cups cider
1 bouquet garni	1 bouquet garni
3 tablespoons water	3 tablespoons water
125 ml./¼ pint double cream	⅝ cup heavy cream
1 tablespoon chopped parsley	1 tablespoon chopped parsley

Melt half the butter in a flameproof casserole, add the chicken and fry until golden brown on all sides. Remove from the pan and put on one side. Peel, core and slice two of the apples, sprinkle with salt and pepper and fry in the butter remaining in the casserole until beginning to brown. Sprinkle in the flour and cook gently, stirring occasionally, until the flour is a pale golden brown. Gradually stir in 250 ml./½ pint (1¼ cups) of the cider and bring to the boil, stirring all the time. Replace the chicken in the casserole and add the bouquet garni. Cover and cook in a moderately hot oven, 190°C, 375°F, Gas Mark 5 for 1 hour.

Shortly before the end of the cooking time, peel, core and quarter the remaining apples. Melt half the remaining butter in the frying pan and fry the apples until lightly browned. Put into an ovenproof dish with the water, cover and put into the oven, under the chicken, until required.

When the chicken is cooked, remove it from the casserole, place on a heated serving dish and keep hot. Add the remaining cider to the juices in the casserole and boil rapidly, uncovered, on top of the stove for about 10 minutes or until well reduced. Strain into a clean pan. Add the quartered apples, cream and the rest of the butter, cut into small pieces. Reheat gently without boiling. Taste and adjust the seasoning and pour the sauce over the chicken. Garnish with the chopped parsley.

Serves 6

Chicken with Tomatoes and Olives

METRIC/IMPERIAL	AMERICAN
4 chicken joints	4 chicken pieces
25 g./1 oz. flour	1/4 cup flour
salt and pepper	salt and pepper
3 tablespoons olive oil	3 tablespoons olive oil
2 onions, chopped	2 onions, chopped
2 garlic cloves, crushed	2 garlic cloves, crushed
400 g./1 lb. tomatoes, peeled	1 lb. tomatoes, peeled
200 g./4 oz. mushrooms sliced	4 oz. mushrooms, sliced
100 g./4 oz. olives	4 oz. olives
1 bouquet garni	1 bouquet garni
pinch of powdered saffron	pinch of powdered saffron
250 ml./1/2 pint white wine	1 1/4 cups white wine
juice of 1 lemon	juice of 1 lemon
2 tablespoons chopped parsley	2 tablespoons chopped parsley

Coat the chicken joints (pieces) with the flour, seasoned with salt and pepper. Heat the oil in a wide, shallow pan and fry the chicken joints for about 8 minutes, or until golden brown all over. Remove from the pan and place in a casserole. Add the onions to the pan and fry for 5 minutes. Add the garlic, tomatoes, mushrooms, olives, bouquet garni, saffron and wine and bring to the boil. Pour over the chicken in the casserole. Cover and cook in a moderate oven, 180°C, 350°F, Gas Mark 4 for 1 hour or until the chicken is tender. Remove the bouquet garni. Stir in the lemon juice and taste and adjust the seasoning. Serve sprinkled with parsley. **Serves 4**

Casseroled Pheasant or Grouse

METRIC/IMPERIAL

1 large pheasant or 2 grouse
25 g./1 oz. butter
1 tablespoon oil
1 large onion, sliced
50 g./2 oz. flour
500 ml./1 pint stock
finely grated rind and juice of
    1 orange
1 tablespoon redcurrant jelly
125 ml./1/4 pint port wine
1 bay leaf
1 parsley sprig
salt and pepper

AMERICAN

1 large pheasant or 2 grouse
2 tablespoons butter
1 tablespoon oil
1 large onion, sliced
1/2 cup flour
2 1/2 cups stock
finely grated rind and juice of
    1 orange
1 tablespoon redcurrant jelly
5/8 cup port wine
1 bay leaf
1 parsley sprig
salt and pepper

Cut the pheasant into four or cut each grouse in half. Heat the butter and oil in a pan and quickly fry the birds on all sides until a good golden colour. Remove from the pan and place in a casserole. Add the onion to the pan and cook until soft. Stir in the flour and cook, stirring, for about 5 minutes, or until golden brown. Gradually add the stock and bring to the boil, stirring all the time. Allow to thicken and add the remaining ingredients. Pour over the pheasant or grouse in the casserole, cover and cook in a warm oven, 170°C, 325°F, Gas Mark 3 for 2 to 4 hours depending on the age of the birds. Taste and adjust the seasoning before serving. **Serves 4**

Pigeons with Redcurrant Jelly

METRIC/IMPERIAL

2 tablespoons oil
8 back bacon rashers
1 onion, finely chopped
4 wood pigeons
4 tablespoons redcurrant jelly
250 ml./1/2 pint stock
1/2 teaspoon grated nutmeg
salt and pepper
200 g./8 oz. green grapes

AMERICAN

2 tablespoons oil
8 lean bacon slices
1 onion, finely chopped
4 wood pigeons
4 tablespoons redcurrant jelly
1 1/4 cups stock
1/2 teaspoon grated nutmeg
salt and pepper
8 oz. green grapes

Heat the oil in a frying pan. Roughly chop half the bacon and add to the pan with the onion. Fry for about 5 minutes. Remove from the pan with a slotted spoon and place in a casserole. Lay a rasher (slice) of bacon over the breast of each pigeon, add the pigeons to the pan and fry on all sides until browned. Add to the casserole. Put the jelly, stock, nutmeg and seasoning into the frying pan and bring just to the boil. Pour over the pigeons in the casserole. Cover and cook in a warm oven, 170°C, 325°F, Gas Mark 3 for 3 hours. Add the grapes and cook for a further 5 minutes. **Serves 4**

Hunters' Casserole

METRIC/IMPERIAL

2 tablespoons oil
200 g./8 oz. streaky bacon,
    chopped
4 onions, chopped
2 carrots, quartered
600 g./1 1/2 lb. venison or
    1 kg./2 1/2 lb. rabbit or hare
40 g./1 1/2 oz. flour
salt and pepper
250 ml./1/2 pint red wine
425 g./15 oz. can tomatoes
1 bay leaf
chopped parsley

AMERICAN

2 tablespoons oil
8 oz. fatty bacon,
    chopped
4 onions, chopped
2 carrots, quartered
1 1/2 lb. venison or
    2 1/2 lb. rabbit or hare
6 tablespoons flour
salt and pepper
1 1/4 cups red wine
15 oz. can tomatoes
1 bay leaf
chopped parsley

Heat the oil in a large pan and fry the bacon, onions and carrots for 10 minutes. Remove from the pan and place in a casserole. Cut the venison into 2 1/2 cm./1 in. cubes, or joint the rabbit or hare. Coat with the flour, seasoned with salt and pepper, and fry in the fat remaining in the pan until brown on all sides. Remove from the pan and add to the vegetables in the casserole. Add the wine, tomatoes, with the juice from the can, and bay leaf to the frying pan. Bring to the boil and pour into the casserole. Cover and cook in a warm oven, 170°C, 325°F, Gas Mark 3 for 2 1/2 hours. Remove the bay leaf, garnish with parsley and serve with boiled rice. **Serves 6**

Hare with Prunes

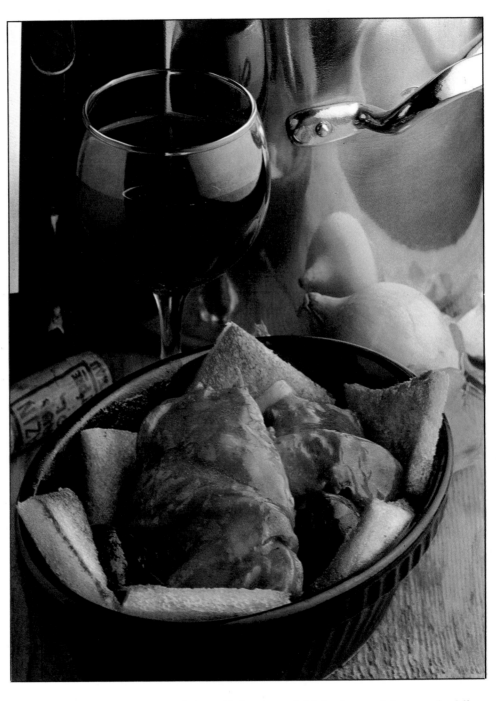

METRIC/IMPERIAL
150 g./6 oz. prunes
250 ml./½ pint red wine
1 hare, with the liver, cut
  into serving pieces
4 tablespoons water
40 g./1½ oz. flour
salt and pepper
75 g./3 oz. dripping
3 onions, chopped
2 garlic cloves, crushed
  (optional)
500 ml./1 pint brown stock
juice of ½ lemon
2 tablespoons redcurrant jelly
1 bouquet garni
2 to 3 slices white bread
25 g./1 oz. butter

AMERICAN
2 cups prunes
1¼ cups red wine
1 hare, with the liver, cut
  into serving pieces
4 tablespoons water
6 tablespoons flour
salt and pepper
⅜ cup dripping
3 onions, chopped
2 garlic cloves, crushed
  (optional)
2½ cups brown stock
juice of ½ lemon
2 tablespoons redcurrant jelly
1 bouquet garni
2 to 3 slices white bread
2 tablespoons butter

Soak the prunes in the red wine overnight. Put the hare liver into a saucepan with the water and simmer gently for 20 minutes or until tender. Mash with the cooking liquid. Coat the hare with the flour, seasoned with salt and pepper.

Heat the dripping in a large flameproof casserole and fry the hare quickly on all sides until golden. Remove from the casserole and put on one side. Fry the onions and garlic, if using, in the fat remaining in the casserole for about 5 minutes or until soft. Stir in any remaining flour, then gradually stir in the stock. Bring slowly to the boil, stirring all the time. Add the lemon juice, mashed liver mixture, redcurrant jelly, prunes, with the wine, and bouquet garni. Season well. Replace the hare in the casserole, cover and cook in a warm oven, 170°C, 325°F, Gas Mark 3 for 3 hours.

Remove the crusts from the bread and cut into triangles. Melt the butter in a frying pan and fry the bread until golden brown on both sides. Taste the hare casserole, adjust the seasoning and remove the bouquet garni. Turn into one large or six to eight smaller serving dishes and garnish with the croûtes. **Serves 6 to 8**

Fish Casseroles

People often choose fish because it can be cooked very quickly, by frying or grilling (broiling), and, unlike meat, you do not have to pay more for quick-cooking cuts. However, fish that is cooked in the oven is generally very moist and full of flavour, so it is well worth trying a fish casserole. Deep freeze owners will find this chapter especially useful as halfway through using large packs of fish steaks or fillets you may run out of different ideas of how to cook them. Once the casserole has been cooked it is also possible to re-freeze it, although I personally do not feel that a fish casserole freezes quite as well as many of the meat casseroles.

Smoked Cod with Corn

METRIC/IMPERIAL
25 g./1 oz. butter
1 small onion, chopped
1 green pepper, seeded and
  chopped
2 tablespoons chopped parsley
326 g./12 oz. can sweetcorn
  kernels, drained
400 to 600 g./1 to 1¼ lb.
  smoked cod fillet
freshly ground black pepper
125 ml./¼ pint single cream

AMERICAN
2 tablespoons butter
1 small onion, chopped
1 green pepper, seeded and
  chopped
2 tablespoons chopped parsley
12 oz. can sweetcorn kernels,
  drained
1 to 1¼ lb. smoked cod fillet
freshly ground black pepper
⅝ cup light cream

Melt the butter in a small pan, add the onion and green pepper and fry for about 8 minutes. Add the parsley and sweetcorn, mix together and turn into a casserole. Cut the cod into four to eight pieces and place on top of the vegetables in the casserole. Season with pepper and pour over the cream. Cover and cook in a moderate oven, 180°C, 350°F, Gas Mark 4 for 30 to 35 minutes.   **Serves 4**
Note: *Do not deep freeze the cooked dish.*

Casseroled Herrings, Country Style

METRIC/IMPERIAL
25 g./1 oz. butter
2 large onions, thinly sliced
100 g./4 oz. streaky bacon,
  chopped
600 g./1½ lb. potatoes, thinly
  sliced
salt and pepper
125 ml./¼ pint milk
4 herrings, cleaned and boned
2 teaspoons French mustard

AMERICAN
2 tablespoons butter
2 large onions, thinly sliced
4 oz. fatty bacon, chopped
1½ lb. potatoes, thinly
  sliced
salt and pepper
⅝ cup milk
4 herrings, cleaned and boned
2 teaspoons French mustard

Melt the butter in a small pan and fry the onions gently for 5 minutes. Add the bacon and fry for a further 5 minutes. Place a third of the potatoes in a greased, ovenproof dish. Cover with half the onion and bacon mixture. Season each layer with salt and pepper. Repeat layers once and finally cover with a layer of potato. Pour over the milk. Cover and bake in a moderately hot oven, 190°C, 375°F, Gas Mark 5 for 1 hour.

Spread the herrings with the mustard and roll up from the head end. Remove the lid from the dish and place the herrings on top of the potatoes. Cover and return to the oven to cook for a further 25 minutes.   **Serves 4**

Piquant Fish Casserole

METRIC/IMPERIAL
2 teaspoons French mustard
4 large or 8 small plaice
  fillets
salt and pepper
25 g./1 oz. butter
150 g./6 oz. mushrooms,
  sliced
1 tablespoon chopped chives
  or spring onions
1 tablespoon chopped parsley
125 ml./1/4 pint single cream

AMERICAN
2 teaspoons French mustard
4 large or 8 small flounder
  fillets
salt and pepper
2 tablespoons butter
6 oz. mushrooms, sliced
1 tablespoon chopped chives
  or scallions
1 tablespoon chopped parsley
5/8 cup light cream

Spread a little of the mustard on one side of each fish fillet and season with salt and pepper. Roll the fillets up, starting at the head and keeping the mustard inside, and place in a shallow casserole.

Melt the butter in a small pan and fry the mushrooms for 2 minutes. Add the chives or spring onions (scallions), parsley, cream and a little seasoning and pour over the fish. Cover and cook in a moderate oven, 180°C, 350°F, Gas Mark 4 for 20 to 30 minutes or until the fish is cooked. **Serves 4**
Note: *Do not freeze the cooked dish.*

Sole with Shrimps

METRIC/IMPERIAL	AMERICAN
200 g./8 oz. potted shrimps	8 oz. potted shrimps
4 large or 8 small fillets of sole	4 large or 8 small fillets of sole
salt and freshly ground black pepper	salt and freshly ground black pepper
2 tablespoons chopped fresh dill or fennel	2 tablespoons chopped fresh dill or fennel
500 ml./1 pint single cream	2½ cups light cream

Cook the shrimps in a saucepan over a very gentle heat until the butter has melted. Strain the butter into a shallow casserole and brush all over the sides. Season the fillets of sole with salt and pepper and divide the shrimps and half the chopped dill or fennel between them. Roll up the fillets and place in the casserole. Pour over the cream and season with more salt and pepper. Cover and cook in a moderately hot oven, 190°C, 375°F, Gas Mark 5 for 20 to 25 minutes or until the fish is cooked. Serve sprinkled with the remaining chopped dill or fennel. **Serves 4**

Fish with Grapes and Peppers

This particular recipe is a very easy one for slimmers.

METRIC/IMPERIAL	AMERICAN
4 to 6 small plaice or whiting fillets	4 to 6 small flounder or whiting fillets
salt and pepper	salt and pepper
125 ml./¼ pint dry cider, white wine or fish stock	⅝ cup dry cider, white wine or fish stock
1 small green pepper, seeded and chopped	1 small green pepper, seeded and chopped
1 small red pepper, seeded and chopped	1 small red pepper, seeded and chopped
50 g./2 oz. green grapes, halved and pipped	⅓ cup halved and seeded green grapes

Season the fish fillets, fold in half and place in an ovenproof dish. Pour over the cider, white wine or fish stock and add the green and red peppers and grapes. Cover and cook in a moderate oven, 180°C, 350°F, Gas Mark 4 for 20 to 30 minutes or until the fish is cooked. **Serves 4**

Note: *Do not freeze this dish.*

Herrings à la Greque

METRIC/IMPERIAL	AMERICAN
4 herrings, cleaned and boned	4 herrings, cleaned and boned
3 tablespoons olive oil	3 tablespoons olive oil
1 onion, grated	1 onion, grated
1 garlic clove, crushed	1 garlic clove, crushed
1 tablespoon tomato purée	1 tablespoon tomato purée
2 teaspoons lemon juice	2 teaspoons lemon juice
salt and pepper	salt and pepper
100 g./4 oz. button mushrooms, sliced	4 oz. button mushrooms, sliced
1 tablespoon chopped parsley	1 tablespoon chopped parsley

Place the herrings in a shallow casserole. Blend the oil, onion, garlic, tomato purée, lemon juice and seasoning together. Add the mushrooms and pour over the herrings. Cover and cook in a moderate oven, 180°C, 350°F, Gas Mark 4 for 30 to 35 minutes or until the herrings are cooked. Serve sprinkled with chopped parsley. **Serves 4**

Trout with White Wine

METRIC/IMPERIAL	AMERICAN
4 trout	4 trout
salt and pepper	salt and pepper
50 g./2 oz. butter	¼ cup butter
1 small onion, very finely chopped	1 small onion, very finely chopped
200 g./8 oz. button mushrooms, finely chopped	8 oz. button mushrooms, finely chopped
2 tablespoons chopped parsley	2 tablespoons chopped parsley
1 tablespoon lemon juice	1 tablespoon lemon juice
125 ml./¼ pint dry white wine	⅝ cup dry white wine

Clean the trout and season inside and out with salt and pepper. Melt the butter in a small pan and fry the onion gently for 5 minutes. Add the mushrooms and cook for a further 2 to 3 minutes, then add the parsley and lemon juice. Use this mixture to stuff the cavity in each fish and place in an ovenproof dish. Pour over the wine, cover and cook in a moderately hot oven, 190°C, 375°F, Gas Mark 5 for 30 minutes. **Serves 4**

Tuna Niçoise

METRIC/IMPERIAL
2 × 198 g./7 oz. cans
   tuna fish
juice of ½ lemon
salt and black pepper
4 anchovy fillets
1 tablespoon olive oil
1 onion, chopped
4 tomatoes, peeled, seeded
   and chopped
1 garlic clove, crushed
1 bouquet garni
125 ml./¼ pint white wine
2 tablespoons chopped parsley

AMERICAN
2 × 7 oz. cans tuna fish
juice of ½ lemon
salt and black pepper
4 anchovy fillets
1 tablespoon olive oil
1 onion, chopped
4 tomatoes, peeled, seeded
   and chopped
1 garlic clove, crushed
1 bouquet garni
⅝ cup white wine
2 tablespoons chopped parsley

Carefully remove the tuna from the cans, so that they stay in shape, and place side by side in an ovenproof dish. Sprinkle them with the lemon juice, season lightly with salt and pepper and arrange the anchovy fillets on the top.

Heat the oil in a small saucepan, add the onion and cook for 5 minutes. Add the tomatoes, garlic, bouquet garni and wine and boil rapidly in the open pan until reduced and thickened. Season to taste, remove the bouquet garni and pour over the tuna. Cover and cook in a moderate oven, 180°C, 350°F, Gas Mark 4 for 15 minutes. Serve sprinkled with the chopped parsley. **Serves 4**

Cornish Casserole

A particularly good dish for those inevitable 'unexpected meals', this makes use of traditional storecupboard and frozen foods and only takes a short time to prepare.

METRIC/IMPERIAL
400 g./1 lb. leeks or onions,
   sliced
200 g./8 oz. potatoes, diced
50 g./2 oz. butter
396 g./14 oz. packet
   frozen cod steaks, diced
425 g./15 oz. can fish
   bisque
100 g./4 oz. frozen peas
salt and pepper

AMERICAN
1 lb. leeks or onions,
   sliced
8 oz. potatoes, diced
¼ cup butter
14 oz. package frozen cod
   steaks, diced
15 oz. can fish bisque
4 oz. frozen peas
salt and pepper

Fry the leeks or onions and potatoes in the butter in a frying pan for 10 minutes. Place in a casserole with the remaining ingredients. Cover and cook in a moderate oven, 180°C, 350°F, Gas Mark 4 for 1 hour. **Serves 4**

Quick Tuna Casserole with Cheese Swirls

METRIC/IMPERIAL

2 × 198 g./7 oz. cans
   tuna fish
1 medium-sized onion,
   chopped
1 large green pepper, seeded
   and chopped
1 garlic clove, crushed
297 g./10½ oz. can
   condensed mushroom soup
125 ml./¼ pint milk
2 tablespoons lemon juice
1 tablespoon chopped parsley
1 tablespoon chopped chives
salt and pepper

For the cheese swirls:
200 g./8 oz. flour
2 teaspoons baking powder
¼ teaspoon salt
pinch of cayenne pepper
50 g./2 oz. butter or
   margarine
about 6 tablespoons milk
100 g./4 oz. Cheddar cheese,
   grated

AMERICAN

2 × 7 oz. cans tuna fish
1 medium-sized onion,
   chopped
1 large green pepper, seeded
   and chopped
1 garlic clove, crushed
10½ oz. can condensed
   mushroom soup
⅝ cup milk
2 tablespoons lemon juice
1 tablespoon chopped parsley
1 tablespoon chopped chives
salt and pepper

For the cheese swirls:
2 cups flour
2 teaspoons baking powder
½ teaspoon salt
pinch of cayenne pepper
¼ cup butter or margarine
about 6 tablespoons milk
1 cup grated Cheddar cheese

Drain off the oil from the tuna into a small saucepan. Fry the onion, green pepper and garlic in this for 5 minutes. Turn into a casserole with the tuna, soup, milk, lemon juice, herbs and seasoning and mix together. Cover and cook in a moderately hot oven, 200°C, 400°F, Gas Mark 6 for 30 minutes.

For the cheese swirls, sift the flour with the baking powder, salt and cayenne pepper. Rub in the butter or margarine until the mixture resembles fine breadcrumbs. Bind together with the milk to give a soft but not sticky dough. Roll out to a rectangle about ¾ cm./¼ in. thick. Sprinkle the surface with grated cheese and roll up like a Swiss (jelly) roll. Seal the edges and cut into slices about ¾ cm./¼ in. thick. Place on a baking sheet and bake above the casserole for 20 minutes. Top the tuna mixture with some of the cheese swirls before serving and serve the rest separately. **Serves 4**

Stuffed Fillets of Plaice (Flounder)

METRIC/IMPERIAL
75 g./3 oz. butter
2 shallots or small onions,
    finely chopped
50 g./2 oz. button mushrooms,
    finely chopped
50 g./2 oz. fresh white
    breadcrumbs
1 tablespoon chopped parsley
pinch of dried rosemary
1 teaspoon grated lemon rind
salt and pepper
2 large plaice fillets
4 streaky bacon rashers
600 g./1½ lb. potatoes
250 ml./½ pint milk

AMERICAN
⅜ cup butter
2 shallots or small onions,
    finely chopped
2 oz. button mushrooms,
    finely chopped
1 cup fresh white
    breadcrumbs
1 tablespoon chopped parsley
pinch of dried rosemary
1 teaspoon grated lemon rind
salt and pepper
2 large flounder fillets
4 fatty bacon slices
1½ lb. potatoes
1¼ cups milk

Melt two-thirds of the butter in a small pan and fry the shallots or onions and mushrooms for 5 minutes. Add the breadcrumbs and cook for a further 5 minutes until crisp, then add the parsley, rosemary, lemon rind and seasoning. Lay one fillet of plaice (flounder) in a large buttered, shallow casserole and season with salt and pepper. Spread the breadcrumb mixture all over it to within 1¼ cm./½ in. of the edge, then cover with the second fillet. Lightly season and top with the rashers (slices) of bacon.

Cook the potatoes in boiling salted water for 10 minutes. Drain and slice. Lay the potato slices all round the fish and pour the milk carefully over them. Cover the casserole and cook in a moderately hot oven, 190°C, 375°F, Gas Mark 5 for 30 minutes. Remove the lid, dot the potatoes with the remaining butter and cook for a further 15 minutes to crisp the bacon and potatoes. **Serves 4**

Cidered Haddock Casserole

METRIC/IMPERIAL
400 g./1 lb. haddock or cod
    fillet
200 g./8 oz. tomatoes, peeled
    and sliced
50 g./2 oz. button mushrooms,
    sliced
1 onion, chopped
1 tablespoon chopped
    parsley
salt and freshly ground
    black pepper
5 tablespoons cider
2 tablespoons fresh white
    breadcrumbs
2 tablespoons grated Cheddar
    cheese

AMERICAN
1 lb. haddock or cod fillet
8 oz. tomatoes, peeled and
    sliced
2 oz. button mushrooms,
    sliced
1 onion, chopped
1 tablespoon chopped parsley
salt and freshly ground
    black pepper
5 tablespoons cider
2 tablespoons fresh white
    breadcrumbs
2 tablespoons grated
    Cheddar cheese

Skin the fish and cut into cubes. Lay the fish cubes in a casserole, cover with the tomatoes, mushrooms and onion, then sprinkle with the parsley and seasoning. Pour over the cider, cover and cook in a moderate oven, 180°C, 350°F, Gas Mark 4 for 20 to 25 minutes or until the fish is cooked. Mix the breadcrumbs and cheese together. Sprinkle over the top of the fish, then put the dish under a hot grill (broiler) until the cheese and breadcrumbs are golden brown. **Serves 4**

Red Mullet (Snapper) Niçoise

METRIC/IMPERIAL
For the stuffing:
1 tablespoon olive oil
1 small onion, finely chopped
1 small garlic clove, crushed
50 g./2 oz. button mushrooms,
    finely chopped
2 tablespoons chopped parsley
salt and pepper

For the fish:
4 red mullet, cleaned
salt and pepper
125 ml./¼ pint dry white wine
few fennel sprigs

AMERICAN
For the stuffing:
1 tablespoon olive oil
1 small onion, finely chopped
1 small garlic clove, crushed
2 oz. button mushrooms,
    finely chopped
2 tablespoons chopped parsley
salt and pepper

For the fish:
4 small red snapper, cleaned
salt and pepper
⅝ cup dry white wine
few fennel sprigs

Heat the oil in a small pan and fry the onion and garlic gently for 5 minutes. Add the mushrooms and cook for a further 2 to 3 minutes, then remove from the heat and add the parsley and seasoning.

Season the fish lightly with salt and pepper inside and out and put a tablespoonful of the stuffing into the stomach cavity of each. Lay the fish in a shallow casserole, pour over the wine and add the sprigs of fennel. Cover and bake in a moderately hot oven, 200°C, 400°F, Gas Mark 6 for 25 minutes or until the mullet (snapper) are cooked. **Serves 4**

Crab and Almonds with Rice

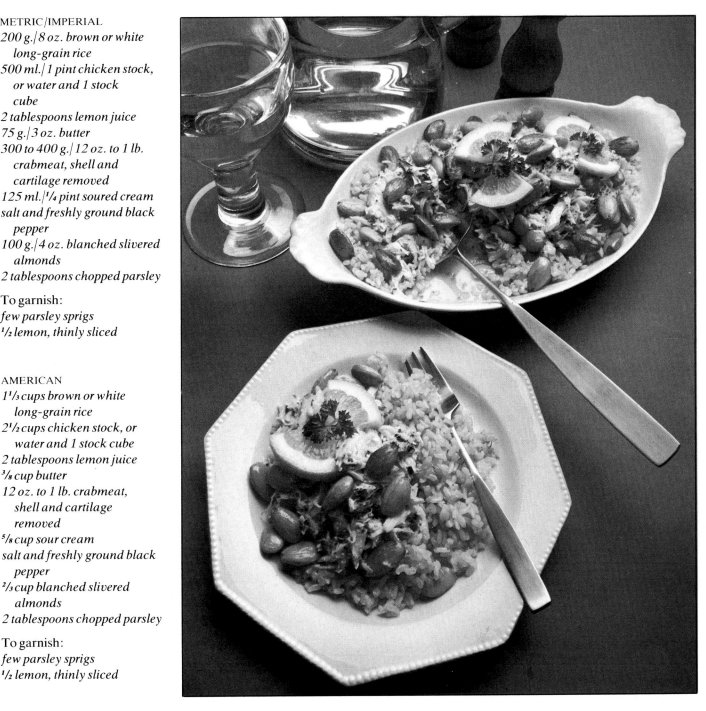

METRIC/IMPERIAL
200 g./8 oz. brown or white
  long-grain rice
500 ml./1 pint chicken stock,
  or water and 1 stock
  cube
2 tablespoons lemon juice
75 g./3 oz. butter
300 to 400 g./12 oz. to 1 lb.
  crabmeat, shell and
  cartilage removed
125 ml./¼ pint soured cream
salt and freshly ground black
  pepper
100 g./4 oz. blanched slivered
  almonds
2 tablespoons chopped parsley

To garnish:
few parsley sprigs
½ lemon, thinly sliced

AMERICAN
1⅓ cups brown or white
  long-grain rice
2½ cups chicken stock, or
  water and 1 stock cube
2 tablespoons lemon juice
⅜ cup butter
12 oz. to 1 lb. crabmeat,
  shell and cartilage
  removed
⅝ cup sour cream
salt and freshly ground black
  pepper
⅔ cup blanched slivered
  almonds
2 tablespoons chopped parsley

To garnish:
few parsley sprigs
½ lemon, thinly sliced

Put the rice, stock or water and stock cube and lemon juice in an ovenproof dish. Cover and cook in a moderate oven, 180°C, 350°F, Gas Mark 4 for 1¼ hours.

Melt two-thirds of the butter in a pan. Add the crabmeat and toss lightly, then stir in the soured cream and seasoning. Spoon over the rice, re-cover and cook for a further 15 minutes. Just before serving, quickly fry the almonds in the remaining butter until they are golden. Sprinkle over the top of the crabmeat and rice with the chopped parsley. Garnish with the parsley sprigs and sliced lemon.   **Serves 4**

Note: *If you want to prepare this dish in advance, the rice can be cooked on top of the stove in a saucepan with the stock and lemon juice for 15 minutes. Turn into a casserole, prepare the crab as above, then re-heat in the oven for 30 minutes before serving. Do not freeze.*

Vegetable Casseroles

Vegetable casseroles fall into two categories: the vegetable side dish which you will serve with a main dish, and the composite vegetable casserole, such as Savoury Stuffed Marrow (Squash), which often forms a complete meal in one pot. These dishes are often fairly cheap as they tend to make the meat, usually the most expensive part of any main dish, 'go further' and the various stuffings given in this chapter can be interchanged or used with other vegetables according to personal taste. There are also very sustaining vegetarian dishes which usually contain peas or beans. The pulses, peas, beans, lentils, etc., have a high protein content and are an economical way of giving the family protein. They can either be used in conjunction with meat or they can provide the entire protein content of a meal.

The increasing cost of fuel has meant that it is more important than ever to use your oven to capacity, and if you are cooking a meat, poultry or game casserole it is also wise to cook the vegetables in the oven at the same time. Unfortunately many vegetables cannot be cooked in this way as they need to be put straight into boiling salted water to retain all their flavour and nutrients. Root vegetables, however, such as carrots and turnips, can be cooked very successfully in the oven and so can some of the more luxury vegetables such as aubergines (eggplants) and courgettes (zucchini). Potatoes baked in their jackets are one of the easiest vegetables of all, so I would recommend cooking potatoes in this way to serve with a casserole. Onions can also be cooked in their skins; this is an old French method from the days when people used to cook their food in the local baker's oven.

Lentils with Salt Pork

METRIC/IMPERIAL	AMERICAN
1 tablespoon oil	1 tablespoon oil
1 onion, chopped	1 onion, chopped
2 garlic cloves, crushed	2 garlic cloves, crushed
1 bouquet garni	1 bouquet garni
1 bay leaf	1 bay leaf
200 g./8 oz. brown or green lentils, soaked overnight and drained	1¹/₃ cups brown or green lentils, soaked overnight and drained
500 ml./1 pint water	2¹/₂ cups water
400 g./1 lb. salt pork, soaked overnight and drained	1 lb. salt pork shoulder butt
salt and freshly ground black pepper	salt and freshly ground black pepper

Heat the oil in a flameproof casserole, add the onion and garlic and fry gently for 5 minutes. Add the bouquet garni, bay leaf, lentils and water and bring to the boil. Add the piece of pork. Cover and cook in a cool oven, 150°C, 300°F, Gas Mark 2 for 2¹/₂ hours. Remove the bouquet garni and bay leaf. Taste and adjust the seasoning. **Serves 4**

Aubergines (Eggplants) Provençale

METRIC/IMPERIAL	AMERICAN
2 large aubergines, thinly sliced	2 large eggplants, thinly sliced
1 tablespoon salt	1 tablespoon salt
olive oil	olive oil
1 large onion, sliced	1 large onion, sliced
1 garlic clove, crushed	1 garlic clove, crushed
200 g./8 oz. tomatoes, peeled and chopped	8 oz. tomatoes, peeled and chopped
1 tablespoon chopped parsley	1 tablespoon chopped parsley
freshly ground black pepper	freshly ground black pepper
25 g./1 oz. fresh white breadcrumbs	¹/₂ cup fresh white breadcrumbs

Put the aubergine (eggplant) slices into a colander, sprinkle with the salt and leave to drain for 30 minutes. Dry well with kitchen paper. Heat a little oil in a large frying pan and fry the aubergine (eggplant) slices, a few at a time, for 2 to 3 minutes on each side, then remove from the pan. Aubergines (eggplants) absorb a great deal of oil in frying, so fry them in the minimum amount of oil. When all the aubergines (eggplants) have been fried, heat 2 tablespoons of oil in the pan and gently fry the onion and garlic for 5 minutes. Add the tomatoes and parsley with plenty of pepper and cook for a further 5 minutes. Put half the aubergines (eggplants) in a casserole, spread over half the tomato mixture, then repeat these layers. Cover and cook in a moderately hot oven, 190°C, 375°F, Gas Mark 5 for 30 minutes. Remove the lid, sprinkle with the breadcrumbs and cook for a further 15 minutes uncovered. Serve hot or cold. **Serves 4 as a side dish**

Chick Pea Casserole

This is an economical vegetarian casserole.

METRIC/IMPERIAL
200 g./8 oz. chick peas,
   soaked overnight and
   drained
salt and pepper
1 tablespoon oil
1 onion, chopped
1 garlic clove, crushed
400 g./1 lb. tomatoes, peeled
   and sliced
200 g./8 oz. cabbage,
   shredded
1 green pepper, seeded and
   chopped
½ teaspoon ground ginger
pinch of ground cloves

AMERICAN
1⅓ cups chick peas
   (garbanzos), soaked
   overnight and drained
salt and pepper
1 tablespoon oil
1 onion, chopped
1 garlic clove, crushed
1 lb. tomatoes, peeled and
   sliced
8 oz. cabbage, shredded
1 green pepper, seeded and
   chopped
½ teaspoon ground ginger
pinch of ground cloves

Put the chick peas in a pan with enough fresh cold water to cover and a little salt. Cover and simmer gently for about 2 hours or until tender.

Heat the oil in a large pan and fry the onion, garlic, tomatoes, cabbage and green pepper for about 10 minutes. Turn into a casserole and add the ginger, cloves and seasoning. Drain the chick peas and reserve the liquid. Add the peas to the vegetables, together with 250 ml./½ pint (1¼ cups) of the pea liquid. Cover and cook in a moderate oven, 180°C, 350°F, Gas Mark 4 for 1 hour. **Serves 4 to 6**

Rice and Bean Casserole

METRIC/IMPERIAL

1 onion, chopped
2 garlic cloves, crushed
1 green pepper, seeded and
    chopped
3 tablespoons oil
400 g./1 lb. long grain rice
3 carrots, diced
200 g./8 oz. green beans,
    fresh or frozen, chopped
400 g./14 oz. can kidney
    beans, drained
1 tablespoon chopped parsley
2 teaspoons salt
pepper
pinch of powdered saffron
1/4 teaspoon ground turmeric
1/4 teaspoon ground coriander
1 tablespoon yeast extract
1 l./2 pints water

AMERICAN

1 onion, chopped
2 garlic cloves, crushed
1 green pepper, seeded and
    chopped
3 tablespoons oil
2 2/3 cups long grain rice
3 carrots, diced
8 oz. green beans, fresh
    or frozen, chopped
14 oz. can kidney beans,
    drained
1 tablespoon chopped parsley
2 teaspoons salt
pepper
pinch of powdered saffron
1/4 teaspoon ground turmeric
1/4 teaspoon ground coriander
1 tablespoon yeast extract
5 cups water

Fry the onion, garlic and green pepper in the oil in a small pan for 5 minutes. Put into a large casserole with the rice, all the vegetables and the parsley. Blend the salt, pepper, saffron, turmeric, coriander and yeast extract with the water. Pour over the vegetables in the casserole and mix well. Cover and cook in a moderate oven, 180°C, 350°F, Gas Mark 4 for 1 1/4 hours.   **Serves 6**

Courgettes (Zucchini) with Tomatoes

METRIC/IMPERIAL
400 g./1 lb. courgettes, sliced
salt and pepper
4 tablespoons olive oil
juice of 1/2 lemon
125 ml./1/4 pint water
1 bay leaf
1 thyme sprig
4 coriander seeds, crushed
1 garlic clove, crushed
4 large tomatoes, peeled

AMERICAN
1 lb. zucchini, sliced
salt and pepper
4 tablespoons olive oil
juice of 1/2 lemon
5/8 cup water
1 bay leaf
1 thyme sprig
4 coriander seeds, crushed
1 garlic clove, crushed
4 large tomatoes, peeled

Put the courgettes (zucchini) slices into a colander, sprinkle with salt and leave to drain for 30 minutes. Put into a casserole with all the remaining ingredients, cover and cook in a moderate oven, 180°C, 350°F, Gas Mark 4 for 1 hour. Taste and adjust the seasoning and either serve hot or allow to cool and serve chilled. **Serves 4 as a side dish**

Savoury Stuffed Cabbage

METRIC/IMPERIAL
For the stuffing:
400 g./1 lb. salt pork belly
25 g./1 oz. butter
1 onion, chopped
2 celery stalks, finely chopped
2 garlic cloves, crushed
100 g./4 oz. crustless white bread
2 tablespoons chopped parsley
1 teaspoon chopped thyme
salt and pepper

For the cabbage:
1 large crisp cabbage, preferably a Savoy
salt
250 ml./1/2 pint well-flavoured stock
1 onion, chopped
2 carrots, chopped
2 leeks, chopped (optional)

AMERICAN
For the stuffing:
1 lb. salt pork fat back
2 tablespoons butter
1 onion, chopped
2 celery stalks, finely chopped
2 garlic cloves, crushed
4 oz. crustless white bread
2 tablespoons chopped parsley
1 teaspoon chopped thyme
salt and pepper

For the cabbage:
1 large crisp cabbage, preferably a Savoy
salt
1 1/4 cups well-flavoured stock
1 onion, chopped
2 carrots, chopped
2 leeks, chopped (optional)

Soak the salt pork for at least 4 hours or overnight in cold water. Drain, dry and remove all the skin and bone. Put through a fairly fine mincer (grinder) or food mill and turn into a bowl. Melt the butter in a small pan and fry the onion, celery and garlic for 5 minutes, then add to the pork. Soak the bread in cold water for 5 minutes, then wring completely dry in your hands. Add to the pork with the remaining stuffing ingredients and blend well.

Leave the cabbage whole, but remove about five of the large outside leaves. Cook both the whole cabbage and the leaves in boiling, salted water for 4 minutes. Drain and rinse in cold water. Very carefully open out the cabbage, leaf by leaf, and starting in the centre spread each leaf with a spoonful of the stuffing. Wrap the large leaves round the cabbage and tie the cabbage securely with string. Pour the stock into a large casserole and add the onion, carrots and leeks, if you are using them. Place the cabbage in the casserole, cover tightly and cook in a warm oven, 170°C, 325°F, Gas Mark 3 for 3 hours. Carefully take the cabbage out of the casserole and remove the string and large cabbage leaves. Arrange on a serving dish with the drained vegetables from the casserole and serve the stock separately. **Serves 6**

French Bean Pot with Sausages

METRIC/IMPERIAL

300 g./12 oz. haricot beans,
  soaked overnight and
  drained
400 g./1 lb. salt pork belly
1 large onion
3 cloves
1 bouquet garni
1 large garlic clove, crushed
400 g./1 lb. pork sausages
15 g./½ oz. bacon dripping or
  lard
70 g./2¼ oz. can tomato
  purée
1 teaspoon sugar
salt and pepper
4 tablespoons fresh white
  breadcrumbs (optional)

AMERICAN

2 cups haricot (dried white)
  beans, soaked overnight
  and drained
1 lb. salt pork fat back
1 large onion
3 cloves
1 bouquet garni
1 large garlic clove, crushed
1 lb. pork sausages
1 tablespoon bacon dripping
  or lard
2¼ oz. can tomato purée
1 teaspoon sugar
salt and pepper
4 tablespoons fresh white
  breadcrumbs (optional)

Put the beans into a large saucepan with the pork, the onion, peeled and studded with the cloves, the bouquet garni and the garlic. Cover with water and bring to the boil. Cover and simmer gently for 1½ hours or until the beans are tender.

Fry the sausages in the bacon dripping or lard until golden brown. Remove from the frying pan and cut each one into three or four pieces. Add the tomato purée to the pan with the sugar and stir over a very gentle heat for 2 to 3 minutes.

When the beans are cooked, lift out the pork and cut it into slices. Drain the beans, reserving the cooking liquid. Discard the bouquet garni and the cloves and chop the onion roughly. Put the beans into a casserole with the pork, onion and sausages. Blend 250 ml./½ pint (1¼ cups) of the reserved bean cooking liquid with the tomato purée mixture in the frying pan and bring to the boil. Season to taste and pour over the beans in the casserole. Mix well and, if necessary, add a little more cooking liquid so that the beans are moist, but not submerged. Sprinkle with the breadcrumbs and bake, uncovered if you want a crisp crust, or cover and bake in a moderate oven, 180°C, 350°F, Gas Mark 4 for 40 minutes. **Serves 4 to 6**

Spinach Niçoise

*A rather unusual vegetable dish, this has the great advantage
that it can be prepared in advance and given the final cooking in
the oven just before you want to serve it.*

METRIC/IMPERIAL
800 g./2 lb. spinach
salt and pepper
75 g./3 oz. butter
3 tablespoons double cream
pinch of grated nutmeg
2 onions, chopped
4 large tomatoes, peeled and
    chopped
100 g./4 oz. Cheddar,
    Gruyère or Emmenthal
    cheese, grated

AMERICAN
2 lb. spinach
salt and pepper
⅜ cup butter
3 tablespoons heavy cream
pinch of grated nutmeg
2 onions, chopped
4 large tomatoes, peeled and
    chopped
1 cup grated Cheddar,
    Gruyère or Emmenthal
    cheese

Wash the spinach well and remove the tough stalks. Bring to
the boil ¾ cm./¼ in. water in a large saucepan with a teaspoon
of salt. Add the spinach and cook for about 10 minutes or until
it is quite tender. Drain well and chop finely. Return to the
pan, stir in half the butter, all the cream, plenty of salt and
pepper and the nutmeg. Put the spinach mixture into a casserole.

Melt the remaining butter in a small pan, add the onions and
fry for 5 minutes. Add the tomatoes and cook gently for a
further 5 minutes. Remove from the heat, stir in the grated
cheese and spoon over the spinach. Cook, uncovered, in a
moderately hot oven, 200°C, 400°F, Gas Mark 6 for 20
minutes or until the tomato mixture is a good golden colour.
Serves 4 to 6

Note: *Do not deep freeze this dish.*

54

Sweet and Sour Red Cabbage

METRIC/IMPERIAL

1 small red cabbage, shredded
2 cooking apples, peeled,
   cored and thinly sliced
2 medium-sized onions,
   thinly sliced
salt and freshly ground black
   pepper
2 tablespoons sugar
2 parsley sprigs
2 small bay leaves
¼ teaspoon dried thyme
2 tablespoons port
2 tablespoons wine vinegar
4 tablespooons soured cream
   (optional)

AMERICAN

1 small red cabbage, shredded
2 cooking apples, peeled,
   cored and thinly sliced
2 medium-sized onions,
   thinly sliced
salt and freshly ground black
   pepper
2 tablespoons sugar
2 parsley sprigs
2 small bay leaves
¼ teaspoon dried thyme
2 tablespoons port
2 tablespoons wine vinegar
4 tablespoons sour cream
   (optional)

Place the cabbage in a casserole in alternate layers with the apples and onions. Season each layer with salt, pepper and sugar. Put the herbs in the middle. Pour over the port and vinegar. Cover and cook in a cool oven, 150°C, 300°F, Gas Mark 2 for 2 hours. If wished, the soured cream can be stirred into the cabbage just before serving. **Serves 4 as a side dish**

Stuffed Peppers in Tomato Sauce

METRIC/IMPERIAL
4 green peppers
salt and pepper
2 tablespoons oil
1 onion, chopped
1 garlic clove, crushed
300 g./12 oz. minced pork
50 g./2 oz. fresh white
* breadcrumbs*
1 egg, lightly beaten
1/4 teaspoon grated nutmeg
pinch of dried sage

For the sauce;
1 tablespoon oil
4 streaky bacon rashers,
* chopped*
1 onion, chopped
425 g./15 oz. can tomatoes
1 tablespoon tomato purée
1/2 teaspoon dried basil
salt and pepper

AMERICAN
4 green peppers
salt and pepper
2 tablespoons oil
1 onion, chopped
1 garlic clove, crushed
12 oz. ground pork
1 cup fresh white breadcrumbs
1 egg, lightly beaten
1/4 teaspoon grated nutmeg
pinch of dried sage

For the sauce;
1 tablespoon oil
4 fatty bacon slices,
* chopped*
1 onion, chopped
15 oz. can tomatoes
1 tablespoon tomato purée
1/2 teaspoon dried basil
salt and pepper

Cut the tops off the peppers and take out the core and seeds. Blanch the peppers, and the lids, in boiling salted water for 1 minute. Drain. Heat the oil in a small pan and fry the onion and garlic for 5 minutes. Remove from the heat, turn into a bowl and add the pork, breadcrumbs, egg, nutmeg and sage. Season well with salt and pepper. Blend together and divide between the four peppers. Top with their lids and place in a small, fairly deep casserole. If necessary cut a small slice off the base of each pepper so that they stand upright.

For the sauce, heat the oil in a pan and fry the bacon and onion for 5 minutes. Add the tomatoes, with the juice from the can, tomato purée, basil and seasoning. Bring to the boil and spoon round the peppers in the casserole. Cover and cook in a moderate oven, 180°C, 350°F, Gas Mark 4 for 1 hour.

Serves 4

Braised Chicory (Endive) with White Sauce

METRIC/IMPERIAL
600 g./1 1/2 lb. chicory heads
25 g./1 oz. butter
1/4 teaspoon grated nutmeg
juice of 1/2 lemon
125 ml./1/4 pint chicken stock,
* or water and 1/4 stock cube*
1 1/2 teaspoons cornflour
1 tablespoon water
2 tablespoons cream
salt and pepper
1 1/2 tablespoons chopped
* parsley*

AMERICAN
1 1/2 lb. French or Belgian
* endive*
2 tablespoons butter
1/4 teaspoon grated nutmeg
juice of 1/2 lemon
5/8 cup chicken stock, or water
* and 1/4 stock cube*
1 1/2 teaspoons cornstarch
1 tablespoon water
2 tablespoons cream
salt and pepper
1 1/2 tablespoons chopped
* parsley*

Wash and trim the chicory (endive), then plunge into boiling water for 1 minute. Drain and rinse in cold water. Drain again. Butter a large casserole and lay the chicory (endive) on the bottom in a single layer. Dot with butter. Stir the nutmeg and lemon juice into the stock, or water and stock cube, and pour over the chicory (endive) in the casserole. Cover and cook in a warm oven, 170°C, 325°F, Gas Mark 3 for 1 1/2 hours.

Blend the cornflour (cornstarch) with the water. Drain the juices from the casserole into a small saucepan, add the cornflour (cornstarch) mixture and bring to the boil, stirring all the time. Allow to boil for 1 minute or until thickened. Remove from the heat, stir in the cream, season to taste and pour over the chicory (endive). Sprinkle with parsley.

Serves 4 as a side dish

Note: *If you do not want to serve the chicory (endive) with a white sauce you can omit this and just serve the vegetable in the casserole with the cooking liquid, sprinkled with parsley.*

Braised Celery

METRIC/IMPERIAL
4 small heads of celery
50 g./2 oz. butter
250 ml./1/2 pint stock
salt and pepper

AMERICAN
4 small heads of celery
1/4 cup butter
1 1/4 cups stock
salt and pepper

Trim and scrub the celery heads, then tie securely with a piece of string to hold their shape. Melt the butter in a flameproof casserole and fry the celery until golden brown on all sides. Add the stock and seasoning. Cover and cook in a moderate oven, 180°C, 350°F, Gas Mark 4 for 1 1/2 hours. Remove the string before serving. **Serves 4 as a side dish**

Cauliflower Basket

This is a very good supper dish to prepare in advance and just heat through in the oven before serving. It is particularly good served with hot crusty granary bread which can be heated in the oven with the cauliflower for 5 minutes.

METRIC/IMPERIAL
1 medium-sized cauliflower
salt and pepper
25 g./1 oz. butter
25 g./1 oz. flour
125 ml./¼ pint milk
150 g./6 oz. Cheddar cheese,
   grated
2 hard-boiled eggs, chopped
1 tablespoon chopped
   gherkins
1 teaspoon capers
1 tablespoon chopped parsley
1 tablespoon chopped chives

AMERICAN
1 medium-sized cauliflower
salt and pepper
2 tablespoons butter
¼ cup flour
⅝ cup milk
1⅓ cups grated Cheddar
   cheese
2 hard-boiled eggs, chopped
1 tablespoon chopped
   gherkins
1 teaspoon capers
1 tablespoon chopped parsley
1 tablespoon chopped chives

Trim the cauliflower, but keep it whole. Cook in boiling salted water for 10 minutes, then drain and reserve the cooking liquid. Melt the butter in a pan, add the flour and cook for 1 minute. Gradually stir in the milk and 125 ml./¼ pint (⅝ cup) of the liquid from cooking the cauliflower. Bring to the boil, stirring all the time. Remove from the heat and stir in almost all the cheese, the eggs, gherkins, capers, parsley, chives and seasoning. Scoop out the centre part of the cauliflower, chop this coarsely and add to the sauce mixture.

Stand the cauliflower in a casserole, pile the cheese sauce mixture in the centre and top with the remainder of the cheese. Cook, uncovered, in a moderately hot oven, 200°C, 400°F, Gas Mark 6 for 30 minutes or until golden brown.

Serves 4

Aubergines (Eggplant) with Garlic

METRIC/IMPERIAL
4 medium-sized aubergines
2 garlic cloves, crushed
1 tablespoon chopped fresh
marjoram
freshly ground black pepper
8 streaky bacon rashers
4 tablespoons olive oil

AMERICAN
4 medium-sized eggplants
2 garlic cloves, crushed
1 tablespoon chopped fresh
marjoram
freshly ground black pepper
8 fatty bacon slices
4 tablespoons olive oil

Make two long slits in each aubergine (eggplant). Press a little crushed garlic, some marjoram and pepper into both sides of each bacon rasher (slice). Stuff a rasher (slice) of bacon into each slit and lay the aubergines (eggplants) in a shallow casserole. Pour over the oil, cover and cook in a warm oven, 170°C, 325°F, Gas Mark 3 for 1½ hours. Remove the lid and cook for a further 30 minutes uncovered. Serve hot or cold.

Serves 4

Savoury Stuffed Peppers

METRIC/IMPERIAL
4 large green peppers
salt
99 g./3½ oz. packet parsley
and thyme stuffing
50 g./2 oz. mushrooms, finely
chopped
1 medium-sized onion, finely
chopped
300 g./12 oz. flaked corned
beef or minced cooked beef
or lamb
1 egg, lightly beaten
50 g./2 oz. butter, melted

AMERICAN
4 large green peppers
salt
3½ oz. envelope parsley and
thyme stuffing
2 oz. mushrooms, finely
chopped
1 medium-sized onion, finely
chopped
12 oz. flaked corned
beef or ground cooked beef
or lamb
1 egg, lightly beaten
¼ cup butter, melted

Cut off the tops from the peppers and remove the cores and seeds. Put the peppers and the tops into a large pan of boiling, salted water and cook for 5 minutes. Drain well. Chop the tops of the peppers finely and put into a bowl with the parsley and thyme stuffing, mushrooms, onion and corned beef or cooked beef or lamb. Mix well and bind together with the egg and butter and water if necessary. Divide the mixture between the four peppers and place in a small, deep casserole. Cover tightly and cook in a moderate oven, 180°C, 350°F, Gas Mark 4 for 30 minutes.

Serves 4

Peas à la Français

METRIC/IMPERIAL
600 g./1½ lb. freshly shelled
or frozen peas
1 lettuce heart, finely
shredded
1 bunch spring onions,
chopped
½ teaspoon salt
freshly ground black pepper
pinch of sugar
50 g./2 oz. butter, melted

AMERICAN
1½ lb. freshly shelled or
frozen peas
1 lettuce heart, finely
shredded
1 bunch scallions, chopped
½ teaspoon salt
freshly ground black pepper
pinch of sugar
¼ cup butter, melted

Put the peas, lettuce, spring onions (scallions), salt, pepper and sugar into a casserole. Pour over the butter and mix lightly. Cover and cook in a moderate oven, 180°C, 350°F, Gas Mark 4 for 1 hour. **Serves 6 as a side dish**

Cucumbers in Cream

METRIC/IMPERIAL
1 large cucumber
salt and freshly ground black
pepper
25 g./1 oz. butter
1 small bunch spring onions,
chopped
½ teaspoon dried dill
4 tablespoons double cream

AMERICAN
1 large cucumber
salt and freshly ground black
pepper
2 tablespooons butter
1 small bunch scallions,
chopped
½ teaspoon dried dill
4 tablespoons heavy cream

Peel the cucumber, then cut into thin strips, about 2½ cm./1 in. long. Put into a colander, sprinkle with salt and leave for 30 minutes for the excess water to drain off. Put into a casserole with the butter, spring onions (scallions), dill and pepper. Cover and cook in a moderate oven, 180°C, 350°F, Gas Mark 4 for 45 minutes, stirring after about 5 minutes when the butter has melted. Stir in the cream, taste and adjust the seasoning and cook for a further 5 minutes. **Serves 4 as a side dish**
Note: *Do not deep freeze this dish.*

Lentil and Vegetable Stew

METRIC/IMPERIAL
200 g./8 oz. orange lentils,
*   soaked overnight and*
*   drained*
1¼ l./2½ pints water
2 onions
2 cloves
1 bay leaf
4 garlic cloves
2 potatoes, coarsely chopped
3 medium-sized courgettes,
*   coarsely chopped*
2 leeks, trimmed and sliced
1 celery stalk, chopped
2 carrots, chopped
1 red pepper, seeded and
*   chopped*
salt and black pepper
1 tablespoon oil
3 tablespoons chopped parsley
juice of 2 lemons

AMERICAN
1⅓ cups orange lentils,
*   soaked overnight and*
*   drained*
6¼ cups water
2 onions
2 cloves
1 bay leaf
4 garlic cloves
2 potatoes, coarsely chopped
3 medium-sized zucchini,
*   coarsely chopped*
2 leeks, trimmed and sliced
1 celery stalk, chopped
2 carrots, chopped
1 red pepper, seeded and
*   chopped*
salt and black pepper
1 tablespoon oil
3 tablespoons chopped parsley
juice of 2 lemons

Put the lentils into a casserole with the water. Stick one of the onions with the cloves and put into the casserole with the bay leaf. Roughly chop two of the garlic cloves and add to the casserole. Cover and cook in a moderate oven, 180°C, 350°F, Gas Mark 4 for 1 hour. Remove the clove-stuck onion and add the potatoes, courgettes (zucchini), leeks, celery, carrots and red pepper. Season to taste, cover and cook for a further 1 hour.

Finely chop the remaining onion and crush the two remaining garlic cloves. Heat the oil in a frying pan and fry the onion and garlic for 5 minutes. Remove the casserole from the oven and add the onion and garlic, the parsley and lemon juice. Remove the bay leaf and taste and adjust the seasoning. Serve either hot or lightly chilled. **Serves 4 to 6**

Vegetable Casserole

METRIC/IMPERIAL

2 tablespoons oil
2 large onions, coarsely
  chopped
2 garlic cloves, crushed
2 green peppers, seeded and
  chopped
400 g./1 lb. courgettes, sliced
2 medium-sized aubergines,
  sliced
200 g./8 oz. mushrooms
400 g./1 lb. tomatoes, peeled
  and sliced
70 g./2 1/4 oz. can tomato
  purée
2 bay leaves
1 tablespoon chopped parsley
1 teaspoon chopped fresh
  marjoram
1 teaspoon chopped fresh
  thyme
salt and pepper
250 ml./1/2 pint stock or water
2 large potatoes, peeled and
  thinly sliced
25 g./1 oz. butter

AMERICAN

2 tablespoons oil
2 large onions, coarsely
  chopped
2 garlic cloves, crushed
2 green peppers, seeded and
  chopped
1 lb. zucchini, sliced
2 medium-sized eggplants,
  sliced
8 oz. mushrooms
1 lb. tomatoes, peeled and
  sliced
2 1/4 oz. can tomato purée
2 bay leaves
1 tablespoon chopped parsley
1 teaspoon chopped fresh
  marjoram
1 teaspoon chopped fresh
  thyme
salt and pepper
1 1/4 cups stock or water
2 large potatoes, peeled and
  thinly sliced
2 tablespoons butter

Heat the oil in a frying pan and fry the onions, garlic and peppers for 5 minutes. Turn into a deep casserole with the courgettes (zucchini), aubergines (eggplants), mushrooms, tomatoes, tomato purée, herbs and seasoning. Pour in the stock or water. Top with the potatoes, dot with the butter and cover. Bake in a moderate oven, 180°C, 350°F, Gas Mark 4 for 1 1/2 hours. Remove the lid and bake for 30 minutes uncovered to brown the potatoes.   **Serves 4**

Cabbage and Tomato Casserole

This is a very good way of using up 'leftover' cabbage.

METRIC/IMPERIAL	AMERICAN
50 g./2 oz. butter	1/4 cup butter
1 medium-sized onion, finely chopped	1 medium-sized onion, finely chopped
1 small cooking apple, peeled, cored and grated	1 small cooking apple, peeled, cored and grated
4 large tomatoes, peeled and chopped	4 large tomatoes, peeled and chopped
1/2 cooked, shredded cabbage	1/2 cooked, shredded cabbage
1 tablespoon chopped parsley	1 tablespoon chopped parsley
salt and pepper	salt and pepper
75 g./3 oz. Cheddar cheese, grated	3/4 cup grated Cheddar cheese
50 g./2 oz. fresh white breadcrumbs	1 cup fresh white breadcrumbs

Melt the butter in a saucepan and gently fry the onion and apple for 5 minutes. Add the tomatoes and cook for a further 5 minutes, then add the cabbage, parsley and seasoning and mix well. Turn into an ovenproof dish and sprinkle with the cheese, mixed with the breadcrumbs. Cook, uncovered, in a moderately hot oven, 200°C, 400°F, Gas Mark 6 for 30 minutes or until the top is golden brown.

Serves 4 as a side dish

Savoury Stuffed Marrow (Squash)

METRIC/IMPERIAL	AMERICAN
1 medium-sized vegetable marrow	1 medium-sized summer squash
15 g./1/2 oz. butter	1 tablespoon butter
200 g./8 oz. minced beef	8 oz. ground beef
100 g./4 oz. pork sausage meat	4 oz. pork sausage meat
25 g./1 oz. fresh white breadcrumbs	1/2 cup fresh white breadcrumbs
1 small onion, grated	1 small onion, grated
1 tablespoon chopped parsley	1 tablespoon chopped parsley
1 tablespoon chopped chives	1 tablespoon chopped chives
1 teaspoon Worcestershire sauce	1 teaspoon Worcestershire sauce
salt and freshly ground black pepper	salt and freshly ground black pepper
1 egg, beaten	1 egg, beaten
For the sauce;	For the sauce:
25 g./1 oz. butter	2 tablespoons butter
25 g./1 oz. flour	1/4 cup flour
250 ml./1/2 pint milk	1 1/4 cups milk
100 g./4 oz. Cheddar cheese, grated	1 cup grated Cheddar cheese
salt and pepper	salt and pepper

Peel the marrow (squash), cut it in half lengthways and scoop out the seeds. Well grease a large, shallow casserole with the butter and lay the two marrow (squash) halves in it side by side. Mix all the remaining ingredients together and use this mixture to stuff both the marrow (squash) halves. Cover and bake in a moderate oven, 180°C, 350°F, Gas Mark 4 for 1 hour.

Melt the butter for the sauce in a small pan. Add the flour and cook, stirring, for 1 minute. Gradually stir in the milk and bring to the boil, stirring all the time, until the sauce thickens. Add the cheese and season to taste with salt and pepper. Remove the lid of the casserole, strain off about half of the liquid in the casserole and pour the cheese sauce over the top. Bake for a further 20 minutes uncovered or until the sauce topping is golden brown.

Serves 4 to 6

Sauerkraut with Knackwurst

METRIC/IMPERIAL	AMERICAN
1 large cooking apple, peeled, cored and grated	1 large cooking apple, peeled, cored and grated
2 carrots, grated	2 carrots, grated
25 g./1 oz. butter, melted	2 tablespoons butter, melted
400 g./1 lb. sauerkraut	1 lb. sauerkraut
1 teaspoon caraway seeds	1 teaspoon caraway seeds
freshly ground black pepper	freshly ground black pepper
4 thick streaky or lean flank bacon rashers	4 thick fatty or lean flank bacon slices
4 knackwurst sausages or 8 frankfurters	4 knackwurst sausages or 8 frankfurters

Mix the apple, carrots, butter, sauerkraut, caraway seeds and pepper together and turn into a casserole. Top with the slices of bacon. Cover and bake in a moderately hot oven, 190°C, 375°F, Gas Mark 5 for 45 minutes. Lay the knackwurst or frankfurters on top and bake uncovered for a further 15 minutes. **Serves 4**

Outlaw Cabbage

METRIC/IMPERIAL	AMERICAN
400 g./1 lb. cooked beef, minced	1 lb. cooked beef, ground
250 ml./½ pint milk	1¼ cups milk
99 g./3½ oz. packet bread sauce mix	3½ oz. envelope bread sauce mix
1 tablespoon tomato purée	1 tablespoon tomato purée
pinch of dried mixed herbs	pinch of dried mixed herbs
1 medium-sized cabbage, shredded	1 medium-sized cabbage, shredded
salt and pepper	salt and pepper
25 g./1 oz. butter	2 tablespoons butter

Put the beef into a mixing bowl. Blend the milk with the bread sauce mix and add to the beef with the tomato purée and herbs. Mix thoroughly and turn into an ovenproof dish. Cover and bake for 25 minutes in a moderate oven, 180°C, 350°F, Gas Mark 4.

Cook the cabbage in boiling, salted water for 5 minutes. Drain, return to the pan and toss lightly with the butter and freshly ground black pepper. Spread over the meat in the dish and bake, uncovered, for a further 10 minutes. **Serves 4 to 6**
Note: *Dry bread sauce mix is used here, but if you prefer you can use 50 g./2 oz. (1 cup) fresh white breadcrumbs.*

Courgettes (Zucchini) with Parsley

METRIC/IMPERIAL	AMERICAN
800 g./2 lb. courgettes, thinly sliced	2 lb. zucchini, thinly sliced
1 teaspoon salt	1 teaspoon salt
50 g./2 oz. butter	¼ cup butter
freshly ground black pepper	freshly ground black pepper
1 tablespoon lemon juice	1 tablespoon lemon juice
2 tablespoons chopped parsley	2 tablespoons chopped parsley

Put the courgettes (zucchini) into a colander. Sprinkle with the salt and leave to drain for 30 minutes, then dry well. Well grease a casserole with some of the butter. Put about a quarter of the courgettes (zucchini) into the casserole, dot with a quarter of the remaining butter and plenty of black pepper, and repeat these layers until all the courgettes (zucchini) and butter have been used. Cover and cook in a moderate oven, 180°C, 350°F, Gas Mark 4 for 1 hour. Remove the casserole from the oven, sprinkle with the lemon juice and parsley and toss lightly together. **Serves 4 to 6 as a side dish**

Cheese, Potato and Onion Casserole

METRIC/IMPERIAL	AMERICAN
1 large onion, thinly sliced	1 large onion, thinly sliced
600 g./1½ lb. potatoes, thinly sliced	1½ lb. potatoes, thinly sliced
200 g./8 oz. Cheddar or Edam cheese, grated	2 cups grated Cheddar or Edam cheese
2 tablespoons chopped parsley	2 tablespoons chopped parsley
salt and freshly ground black pepper	salt and freshly ground black pepper
125 ml./¼ pint milk	⅝ cup milk

Put a layer of onion in a casserole, cover with a layer of potatoes and sprinkle with some of the cheese, parsley and seasoning. Repeat these layers ending with a layer of cheese. Pour over the milk, cover and bake in a moderate oven, 180°C, 350°F, Gas Mark 4 for 1¾ hours. Remove the lid of the casserole and bake for a further 15 minutes to allow the cheese and potatoes to become golden brown. **Serves 4**

Spinach Stuffed Tomatoes

METRIC/IMPERIAL
6 large tomatoes
400 g./1 lb. spinach
salt and pepper
50 g./2 oz. butter
2 to 3 tablespoons pine nuts
2 garlic cloves, crushed

AMERICAN
6 large tomatoes
1 lb. spinach
salt and pepper
¼ cup butter
2 to 3 tablespoons pine nuts
2 garlic cloves, crushed

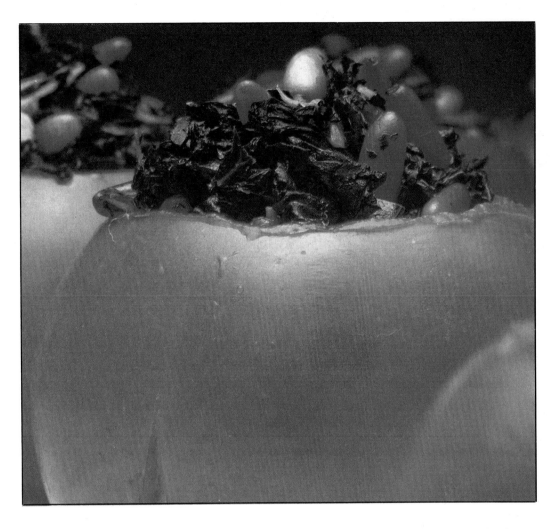

Cut off the tops from the tomatoes and scoop out the pulp. This can be kept to use as a flavouring for another casserole or soup. Turn the tomatoes upside down on a plate or board and leave to drain while preparing the spinach.

Wash the spinach and remove any coarse stalks. Bring to the boil ¾ cm./¼ in. water in a pan with a teaspoon of salt. Add the spinach and cook for 7 to 10 minutes or until just tender. Drain well and either chop finely or blend in a liquidizer to a smooth purée. Melt the butter in a small pan and fry the pine nuts and garlic for 2 to 3 minutes. Add to the spinach, mix well and season to taste. Spoon the spinach mixture into the tomato cases and stand in a small shallow casserole. Cover and cook in a moderate oven, 180°C, 350°F, Gas Mark 4 for 20 to 30 minutes or until the tomatoes are heated through, but not too soft.   **Serves 6**

Note: *Do not deep freeze this dish.*

Savoury Stuffed Mushrooms

METRIC/IMPERIAL
8 large mushrooms
2 to 3 tomatoes, peeled and
  chopped
1 small onion, grated
40 g./1½ oz. softened butter
1 tablespoon chopped parsley
½ teaspoon chopped fresh
  thyme
salt and pepper

AMERICAN
8 large mushrooms
2 to 3 tomatoes, peeled and
  chopped
1 small onion, grated
3 tablespoons softened butter
1 tablespoon chopped parsley
½ teaspoon chopped fresh
  thyme
salt and pepper

Remove the stalks from the mushrooms and chop finely. Mix together with the tomatoes, onion, 25 g./1 oz. (2 tablespoons) of the softened butter, the parsley, thyme and seasoning and blend well. Place the mushroom caps on a large, lightly greased, shallow ovenproof dish or plate. Divide the stuffing between them and dot with the remaining butter. Cover and cook in a moderate oven, 180°C, 350°F, Gas Mark 4 for 20 to 30 minutes.   **Serves 4 as a side dish**

Note: *Do not deep freeze this dish.*

Oven-cooked Risotto

METRIC/IMPERIAL	AMERICAN
200 g./8 oz. long grain rice	1⅓ cups long grain rice
300 to 400 g./12 oz. to 1 lb. meat (see right), chopped	12 oz. to 1 lb. meat (see right), chopped
2 onions, sliced	2 onions, sliced
200 g./8 oz. frozen mixed vegetables	8 oz. frozen mixed vegetables
1 teaspoon curry powder	1 teaspoon curry powder
1 tablespoon soy sauce	1 tablespoon soy sauce
salt and pepper	salt and pepper
500 ml./1 pint water	2½ cups water
100 g./4 oz. Cheddar cheese, grated	1 cup grated Cheddar cheese

Put the rice, meat, onions and mixed vegetables into a casserole and mix together. Put the curry powder, soy sauce and seasoning into a measuring jug and add the water. Stir well, then stir into the rice mixture in the casserole. Cover and cook in a moderate oven, 180°C, 350°F, Gas Mark 4 for 1½ hours. Serve sprinkled with the grated cheese. **Serves 4**

Note: *You can use any meat you like, so long as it will be tender in 1½ hours. It is an excellent way of using up leftover cooked meat, such as lamb and pork, or it is very good with sausages, frankfurters, or tinned pork luncheon meat.*

Sausage and Red Cabbage Casserole

METRIC/IMPERIAL	AMERICAN
400 g./1 lb. red cabbage, finely shredded	1 lb. red cabbage, finely shredded
1 large onion, sliced	1 large onion, sliced
4 tablespoons cider or distilled malt vinegar	4 tablespoons cider or distilled malt vinegar
1 tablespoon Demerara sugar	1 tablespoon light brown sugar
25 g./1 oz. butter	2 tablespoons butter
400 g./1 lb. pork sausages	1 lb. pork sausages
200 g./8 oz. cooking apples, peeled and chopped	8 oz. cooking apples, peeled and chopped
1 to 2 tablespoons sultanas (optional)	1 to 2 tablespoons seedless raisins (optional)
125 ml./¼ pint stock	⅝ cup stock
grated rind of 1 small orange	grated rind of 1 small orange
1 bay leaf	1 bay leaf
¼ teaspoon grated nutmeg	¼ teaspoon grated nutmeg
salt and pepper	salt and pepper

Put the cabbage into a casserole with the onion. Mix together the vinegar and sugar and pour over the cabbage. Heat the butter in a frying pan and fry the sausages gently until golden brown. Set the sausages aside and pour the fat over the cabbage. Add the apples, sultanas (raisins), stock, grated orange rind, bay leaf, nutmeg and seasoning to the cabbage in the casserole. Mix well. Cover and cook in a moderate oven, 180°C, 350°F, Gas Mark 4 for 1 hour. Taste and adjust the seasoning, lay the sausages on top and continue cooking, covered, for a further 30 minutes. **Serves 4**

Dolmades

METRIC/IMPERIAL	AMERICAN
425 g./15 oz. can vine leaves	15 oz. can vine leaves
3 tablespoons oil, preferably olive	3 tablespoons oil, preferably olive
2 medium-sized onions, sliced	2 medium-sized onions, sliced
1 garlic clove, crushed (optional)	1 garlic clove, crushed (optional)
400 g./1 lb. lean cooked beef or lamb, minced	1 lb. lean cooked beef or lamb, ground
1 tablespoon chopped parsley	1 tablespoon chopped parsley
4 tablespoons cooked long grain rice	4 tablespoons cooked long grain rice
2 tablespoons tomato purée	2 tablespoons tomato purée
juice of 1 lemon	juice of 1 lemon
salt and pepper	salt and pepper
4 tablespoons water	4 tablespoons water

Drain the vine leaves and soak in boiling water for 1 to 2 minutes. Drain well in a colander and leave to dry while preparing the stuffing. The vine leaves are very delicate so you must take care that they do not break and tear during this process.

Heat 2 tablespoons of the oil in a pan, add the onions and garlic, if using, and fry for 5 minutes. Add the meat, parsley, rice and half the tomato purée. Continue cooking gently for a further 5 minutes. Remove from the heat, stir in the lemon juice and season to taste. Lay the vine leaves out flat on a board and put a tablespoon of the stuffing on each leaf. Roll up, tucking in the sides to make a neat roll. Arrange the rolls in a casserole. Mix the remaining tomato purée and oil with the water and pour over the rolls. Cover and cook in a moderate oven, 180°C, 350°F, Gas Mark 4 for 45 minutes. **Serves 4**

Boston Baked Beans

This is a traditional American recipe.

METRIC/IMPERIAL
600 g./1½ lb. haricot beans,
* soaked overnight and*
* drained*
salt and pepper
800 g./2 lb. belly pork
2 tablespoons black treacle or
* molasses*
2 teaspoons dry mustard
2 onions, finely chopped

AMERICAN
1½ lb. haricot (dried white)
* beans, soaked overnight*
* and drained*
salt and pepper
2 lb. salt pork
2 tablespoons black treacle
* or molasses*
2 teaspoons dry mustard
2 onions, finely chopped

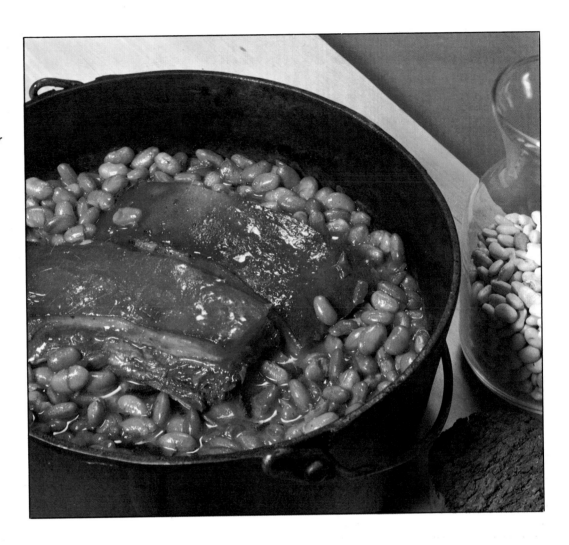

Put the beans into a pan with fresh cold water to cover and a little salt and bring to the boil. Cover and simmer gently for 1 hour. Drain and reserve the liquid.

Score the rind of the pork, and cut the pork into two pieces. Place one piece at the bottom of a large casserole. Add the beans and bury the remainder of the pork in the beans so that the rind just shows. Stir the treacle or molasses, mustard, onions and pepper into the reserved liquid from the beans and pour over the beans in the casserole. Add more water if necessary to cover the beans. Cover the casserole and cook in a cool oven, 150°C, 300°F, Gas Mark 2 for 3 hours. Check the casserole from time to time to make sure the beans are still quite moist, and if necessary add a little extra boiling water.

Remove the lid from the casserole, bring the pork to the surface and cook uncovered for 1 hour to crisp the rind of the pork.   **Serves 4 to 6**

Oven-cooked Carrots

METRIC/IMPERIAL
400 g./1 lb. carrots, thinly
* sliced*
4 tablespoons water
25 g./1 oz. butter
pinch of sugar
salt and pepper
1 tablespoon chopped parsley

AMERICAN
1 lb. carrots, thinly
* sliced*
4 tablespoons water
2 tablespoons butter
pinch of sugar
salt and pepper
1 tablespoon chopped parsley

Put the carrots into a casserole with the water, butter, sugar and seasoning. Cover tightly and cook in a moderate oven, 180°C, 350°F, Gas Mark 4 for 1½ hours or until the carrots are tender. Serve sprinkled with the parsley.

Serves 4 as a side dish

Fruit Casseroles

These are some of the simplest of all sweet dishes to prepare and most of the recipes given in this chapter have a slightly unusual flavour variation, such as Gooseberries in Ginger Beer. For many of these recipes you can either use fresh fruit when it is cheap and in season or you can use frozen fruit. Packs of unsweetened fruit, such as rhubarb, gooseberries and plums, can be bought from freezer centres and these are particularly good for using in these dishes.

Most fruit casseroles are just as good served hot or cold, so in some cases you may feel that you want to double the quantities so that you can serve it hot one day and cold the next. If you do not want to go to the expense of serving fresh cream, remember that ice cream goes just as well with hot cooked fruit as it does with cold – in fact I think it is nicer!

Fruit that is cooked in the oven should not be cooked at a temperature higher than 170°C, 325°F, Gas Mark 3 as it tends to break up and become over-cooked. This is the temperature I have given for most of the recipes. If you are cooking something else in the oven at a lower temperature, allow a slightly longer cooking time for the fruit casserole.

Dried Apricots with Almonds

METRIC/IMPERIAL	AMERICAN
200 g./8 oz. dried apricots	8 oz. dried apricots
375 ml./¾ pint water	2 cups water
50 g./2 oz. sugar	¼ cup sugar
1 vanilla pod or few drops vanilla essence	1 vanilla pod or few drops vanilla extract
50 g./2 oz. blanched split almonds	¼ cup blanched split almonds

Put the dried apricots into a small casserole with the water and leave to soak for 1 hour. Add the sugar and the vanilla pod or vanilla essence (extract). Cover the casserole and cook in a cool oven, 150°C, 300°F, Gas Mark 2 for 1¾ hours. Add the almonds and cook for a further 15 minutes. Remove the vanilla pod before serving. Serve either hot or cold. **Serves 4**

Plums with Port

METRIC/IMPERIAL	AMERICAN
800 g./2 lb. plums	2 lb. plums
100 g./4 oz. brown sugar	⅔ cup brown sugar
125 ml./¼ pint port wine	⅝ cup port wine

Cut the plums in half and take out the stones. Put into a casserole, sprinkle over the sugar and pour the port over the top. Cover and cook in a cool oven, 150°C, 300°F, Gas Mark 2 for 45 minutes to 1 hour, or until the plums are tender.

This dish can be served hot, but is even more delicious if it is served lightly chilled with whipped cream. **Serves 4 to 6**

Baked Apples with Cider

METRIC/IMPERIAL	AMERICAN
4 eating apples	4 eating apples
2 tablespoons dried mixed fruit	2 tablespoons dried mixed fruit
2 tablespoons golden syrup	2 tablespoons light corn syrup
250 ml./½ pint sweet cider	1¼ cups sweet cider

Peel and core the apples, but leave them whole. Mix the dried fruit with the golden (light corn) syrup, then use this mixture to stuff the centre of each apple. Place in a small casserole, pour over the cider and cover. Cook in a warm oven, 170°C, 325°F, Gas Mark 3 for 1 hour. Serve either hot or cold. **Serves 4**

Rhubarb with Orange and Honey

METRIC/IMPERIAL
600 g./1½ lb. rhubarb
grated rind and juice of 1 large
* orange*
4 tablespoons clear honey

AMERICAN
1½ lb. rhubarb
grated rind and juice of
* 1 large orange*
4 tablespoons clear honey

Wipe the rhubarb with a clean cloth, trim off the ends and cut into 2½ cm./1 in. pieces. Put into a casserole with the orange rind and juice and the honey. Cover and cook in a warm oven, 170°C, 325°F, Gas Mark 3 for 45 minutes to 1 hour, or until the rhubarb is tender. **Serves 4**

Bananas with Oranges

METRIC/IMPERIAL
50 g./2 oz. butter
2 tablespoons soft brown sugar
finely grated rind and juice of
* 1 orange*
juice of ½ lemon
pinch of ground mixed spice
4 large bananas
2 tablespoons desiccated
* coconut*

AMERICAN
¼ cup butter
2 tablespoons soft brown sugar
finely grated rind and juice of
* 1 orange*
juice of ½ lemon
pinch of ground allspice
4 large bananas
2 tablespoons shredded
* coconut*

Melt the butter in a pan with the brown sugar, orange rind and juice, lemon juice and mixed spice. Peel the bananas, split them in half lengthways and place in a casserole. Pour over the butter mixture, sprinkle with the coconut and bake in a moderate oven, 180°C, 350°F, Gas Mark 4 for 30 minutes. Serve hot or cold. **Serves 4**

Gooseberries in Ginger (Root) Beer

METRIC/IMPERIAL
600 g./1½ lb. gooseberries
50 to 100 g./2 to 4 oz. sugar
250 ml./½ pint ginger beer
25 g./1 oz. crystallized ginger,
* finely chopped*

AMERICAN
1½ lb. gooseberries
¼ to ½ cup sugar
1¼ cups root beer
⅓ cup finely chopped
* crystallized ginger*

Top and tail the gooseberries and place in a casserole. Sprinkle with the sugar; the amount of sugar required will depend on the type of gooseberries and the time of year. Pour over the ginger (root) beer. Cover the casserole and cook in a warm oven, 170°C, 325°F, Gas Mark 3 for 45 minutes to 1 hour or until the gooseberries are tender. Sprinkle with the crystallized ginger before serving. **Serves 4**

Casseroled Pears with Prunes

METRIC/IMPERIAL
200 g./8 oz. prunes
250 ml./½ pint wine or cider
400 g./1 lb. small pears,
* peeled, cored and quartered*
grated rind and juice of 1
* orange*
100 g./4 oz. sugar

AMERICAN
8 oz. prunes
1¼ cups wine or cider
1 lb. small pears, peeled,
* cored and quartered*
grated rind and juice of 1
* orange*
½ cup sugar

Soak the prunes overnight or for several hours in the wine or cider in a casserole. Add the pears to the casserole with the grated orange rind and juice and the sugar. Cover and cook in a warm oven, 170°C, 325°F, Gas Mark 3 for 1 hour or until the pears and prunes are quite tender. Either serve hot or allow to become cold and then chill. Serve with cream. **Serves 4 to 6**

Plum Crunch

METRIC/IMPERIAL
800 g./2 lb. plums
100 g./4 oz. Demerara sugar
50 g./2 oz. Rice Krispies or
* cornflakes, lightly crushed*

AMERICAN
2 lb. plums
⅔ cup light brown sugar
1½ cups Rice Krispies or
* cornflakes, lightly crushed*

Cut the plums in half and remove the stones. Place in a shallow casserole and sprinkle with the sugar mixed with the crushed Rice Krispies or cornflakes. Bake in a moderately hot oven, 190°C, 375°F, Gas Mark 5 for 45 minutes. Serve with cream. **Serves 4 to 6**

Apples and Pears in Red Wine

METRIC/IMPERIAL	AMERICAN
75 g./3 oz. sugar	3/8 cup sugar
250 ml./1/2 pint water	1 1/4 cups water
250 ml./1/2 pint red wine	1 1/4 cups red wine
1/4 teaspoon ground cinnamon	1/4 teaspoon ground cinnamon
2 tablespoons redcurrant jelly	2 tablespoons redcurrant jelly
4 dessert pears	4 dessert pears
4 dessert apples	4 dessert apples

Put the sugar, water, wine, cinnamon and redcurrant jelly into a flameproof casserole and heat gently until the sugar and jelly have dissolved. Peel the pears, but leave whole with the stalk intact. Add to the casserole, cover and cook in a warm oven, 170°C, 325°F, Gas Mark 3 for 20 minutes. Prepare the apples in the same way as the pears and add to the casserole. Cook for 20 minutes longer.

Take the apples and pears out of the casserole and place in a serving dish. Boil the cooking liquid rapidly until it is reduced to a thin syrup. Pour over the fruit, allow to cool and then chill.

Serves 4

Apple Bake

METRIC/IMPERIAL
800 g./2 lb. cooking apples,
    peeled, cored and sliced
2 tablespoons water
100 g./4 oz. Demerara sugar
50 g./2 oz. cornflakes
2 tablespoons desiccated
    coconut
finely grated rind of 1 lemon
25 g./1 oz. butter

AMERICAN
2 lb. cooking apples,
    peeled, cored and sliced
2 tablespoons water
²/₃ cup light brown sugar
1 cup cornflakes
2 tablespoons shredded
    coconut
finely grated rind of 1 lemon
2 tablespoons butter

Put the apples into a saucepan with the water and half the sugar. Cover and cook over a gentle heat until the apples are soft. Either turn into four individual ovenproof dishes or one large one. Mix together the cornflakes, coconut, remaining sugar and lemon rind. Sprinkle over the apples. Dot with the butter. Bake the small individual dishes in a moderately hot oven, 170°C, 375°F, Gas Mark 5 for 20 minutes or the large dish for 40 minutes.   **Serves 4**

Dried Fruit and Nut Salad

METRIC/IMPERIAL
100 g./4 oz. prunes
100 g./4 oz. dried apricots
100 g./4 oz. dried figs
50 g./2 oz. raisins
750 ml./1½ pints water
25 g./1 oz. shelled walnuts
25 g./1 oz. blanched almonds
25 g./1 oz. pine nuts
    (optional)

AMERICAN
⅔ cup prunes
⅔ cup dried apricots
⅔ cup dried figs
⅓ cup raisins
3¾ cups water
3 tablespoons shelled
    walnuts
3 tablespoons blanched
    almonds
3 tablespoons pine nuts
    (optional)

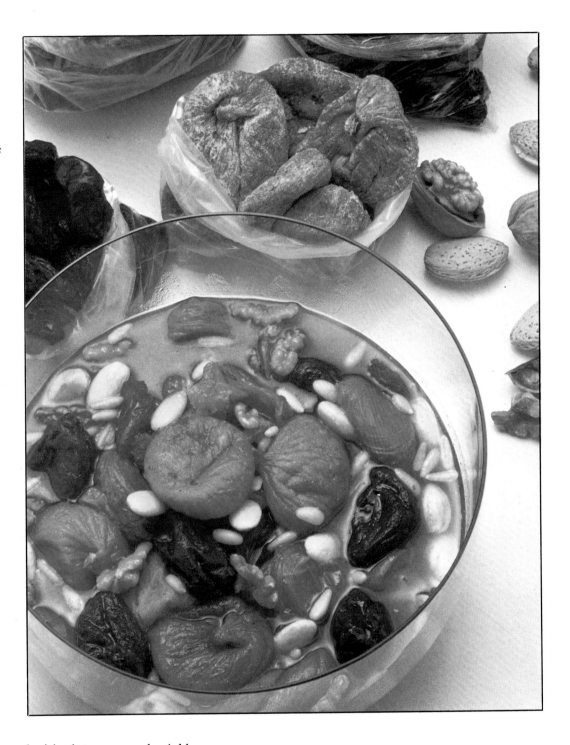

Put the prunes, apricots, figs and raisins into a casserole. Add
the water and leave to soak overnight. Cover and cook in a
cool oven, 150°C, 300°F, Gas Mark 2 for 1 hour. Add the nuts.
Allow to cool, and then chill.   **Serves 6 to 8**

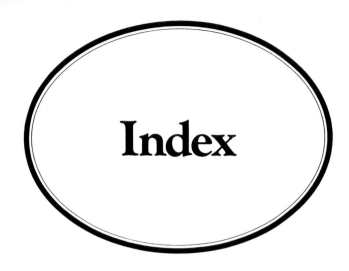

Index

Acknowledgments

The publishers gratefully acknowledge the use of photographs from the follow
sources: Argentine Beef Bureau 6; Bryce Attwell 39; California Prune Advis
Bureau 8; Colman's Mustard 9; Eden Vale Ltd 34; Electricity Council 33; Fr
Producers' Council 23, 36, 69; John West Foods Ltd 44, 45; Kellogg Co of Great Britain
Michael Leale 10, 35, 42; John Lee 20-21, 54, 57, 61; National Dairy Council
National Magazine Co Ltd 34; *New Idea* Magazine 7; New Zealand Lamb Informati
Bureau 21; Norman Nicholls 13, 15, 16, 17, 18, 26, 32, 47, 50, 51, 52, 55, 59, 60, 63, 65,
Olives from Spain 22; Pentangle Photography 37; Roger Phillips 2-3, 4, 30-31, 40-41, 48-
66-67; RHM Foods 25; Sausage Advisory Bureau 53.